Business Lessons for Entrepreneurs

35 THINGS I LEARNED BEFORE THE AGE OF THIRTY

MARK D. CSORDOS

THOMSON
™

Australia · Canada · Mexico · Singapore · Spain · United Kingdom · United States

THOMSON
™

Business Lessons for Entrepreneurs
By Mark D. Csordos

Editor-in-Chief
Jack Calhoun

**Vice President/
Executive Publisher**
Dave Shaut

Acquisitions Editor
Steve Momper

**Channel Manager,
Retail**
Bari Shokler

**Channel Manager,
Professional**
Mark Linton

Production Editor
Alan Biondi

Production Manager
Tricia Matthews Boies

**Manufacturing
Coordinator**
Charlene Taylor

Copy Editor:
Karen Davis

Compositor
Carlisle
Communications, Ltd.

Printer
Transcontinental
Peterborough, Ontario

Internal Designer
Mike Stratton

Cover Designer
Mike Stratton

ISBN: 0-538-72649-0

TABLE OF CONTENTS

ACKNOWLEDGMENTS

First and above all else I would like to thank my wife, Denise, for her tremendous support. Never once has she doubted we would make it. We share a common vision and bond.

To my sweetheart, Amanda. The best part of my day is looking at you when you wake up and seeing your beautiful smile. You are truly a gift.

To Mom, Dad, Scott, and Janeen. I love you all very much and I appreciate your belief in me. I hope any success I achieve can be shared with all of you. I could not ask for a better family. A special thanks to Janeen for all of her input.

To my dear friends Jim, Kevin, and Alex. What can I say? True friends are rare gems. Thanks for seeing the potential in me when I was just some kid in sweatpants packing out groceries.

To Willy Campbell, for taking the time to help mentor me and send me in the right directions, and also for writing the foreword to this book.

To all the people everywhere, no matter what field they are in, who wake up each morning and try to make the world they touch a better place.

Last but not least, thank you Neece E. Bum.

FOREWORD

Business success is about people . . . not about things. It is about understanding what motivates people to act: why, when, how, where do they do such and such . . . or don't do such and such. General Electric's CEO Jack Welch understood this better than any counterpart and that is why GE is the paradigm of the corporate world.

Gaining the knowledge of these secrets can take a lifetime . . . or you can read Mark Csordos. He has the unique ability to stand back and make a perceptive appraisal of events and of how the people involved caused the events to unfold. Understanding motivation is fundamental to establishing a successful business . . . and to successfully running a business.

And it is fundamental to any size of business. You are an entrepreneur even in the corporate world. If you are part of a large organization, you are responsible for a specific part of the whole . . . "your business" . . . and you are dealing with people. You need to know what to look for, what to expect, and how to turn events to your direction.

I have seen "old timers" light up at Mark's seminars with recognition of Mark's candid portrayal of customers, bosses, secretaries and spouses . . . and why they do what they do. I have seen budding entrepreneurs smile with appreciation as he demonstrated an insight with a real world experience.

Understanding your own strengths and weaknesses is one of the keys to your success that you will have to do yourself. With the tools that Mark will give you, you can handle that one too, as well as bring a much more experienced approach to the world of business.

William H. Campbell
SCORE Counselor and retired aerospace executive

HOW TO USE THIS BOOK

When you read this book, I want it to be just as if I was sitting across from you at lunch giving you the straightforward advice I wish I had before I started my company. These thirty-five lessons are from my own experiences and ones that I feel will greatly increase your knowledge in entrepreneurship. They especially offer advice on what it's like to be a new entrepreneur. Your Introduction to Business course book doesn't include a chapter on "Watch Out for Number One" or "Let's Face It: People Lie to You." I wish I had been prepared for some of the harsher aspects of the business world.

I also don't want to insult my readers' intelligence. I have read other entrepreneur books and I feel that my readers are smart enough to know to look presentable in meetings, wear clean clothes, and have professional business cards. I assume you know basic business etiquette and I won't waste your time rehashing the obvious.

In several chapters, such as "Learn the Art of Self Promotion," I include tips to get you started moving in the right direction. In the four years I owned my own business, I did my own PR for less than $1,000 total. I had no experience or connections, but my company appeared in over two dozen articles, including *The New York Times* twice and *Vogue*. I guarantee that if you follow those ten tips you will get publicity for your company.

In the end, I hope you not only enjoy the book, but that it saves you time and money. Feel free to abuse this book. All of my favorite books are heavily highlighted, with notes written all over the pages. This book was also written so that you don't have to read it from front to back. I know how time challenged I am, and I find it helpful when I can pick and choose what I want to read and then go back and read the other chapters when I have more time.

To all of my readers, thank you for purchasing my book. I would like to wish you all a heartfelt, "Good luck and much success." Other than the birth of my daughter, my most satisfying accomplishment was running my own business.

INTRODUCTION

MY STORY

The idea for this book came in a roundabout way. When I was preparing to sell my business I started to reflect on the previous four years, where I had come from, and what I had learned. I decided that when I finished selling my company, I was going to make a list of everything I did wrong so that I would not repeat those mistakes with any companies I would start in the future. As I began to write, though, the list developed more into the lessons I learned rather than the mistakes I made. As I added commentary to the list, this book idea started to take shape. I decided that I wanted to write the book that I wish **I'd had** when I was just starting out. I think I did that. I hope you find this book helpful. It is all culled from my personal experiences, from the time I started the business from scratch, until the time it was sold.

My background is unspectacular. As Thomas Edison said of genius, it's ". . . ninety-nine percent perspiration and one percent inspiration." I'm no genius, but I do work hard and I don't give up. I attended three colleges and wound up with a Communications degree from Rutgers University. I had only average grades because I worked full time throughout college. I missed a lot of social events at school, but the hard work paid off. I owed nothing in student loans and my last semester of school I purchased a house. Somewhere in there I found time to date and met my wife at the tail end of my college career. We were driving in the car one day early in our relationship, and we joked that someday we would start our own company and she would be the vice president. We did and she was.

I met my credit requirements for Rutgers in the summer of 1994 and officially graduated with the spring class in 1995. I had worked for A&P (a supermarket chain) since I was 16 and at the time of graduation I was working full time and making decent money, but I had a dead-end job. If I had stayed with them I would have done the same exact job for the next twenty years. I wanted to own my own business, but I didn't know what type. What was I qualified to do? I had read a lot of business magazines, and I stumbled across one paragraph about mystery shopping. I said, "I could do that." I asked my fiancée and my best friend what they thought about the idea. They thought we could do it. Just that easily, C&S Mystery Shoppers was born.

First, I'll have to brief you on mystery shopping, since that's the first question most people ask me. Mystery shopping is very simple. "Shoppers" as they are called, go into a client's establishment posing as regular customers and rate their customer service experiences based on certain predetermined criteria. The information gets written in a report form and is then sent back to that company's management. It gives the owners and management an objective look at their operations. It tells them how customers are being treated. Our first client was Pizza Hut. I'll take you on a sample "shop." My wife and I would go to a Pizza Hut at 6:00 PM on Saturday dressed in jeans and T-shirts. We were just another couple going out for dinner. (Obviously, the employees being evaluated did not know we were mystery shoppers.) We would note the time we arrived at the restaurant and how long it took to get greeted. Then we would note how long it took the waitress to come to the table, always making sure to get names of employees we interact with. The waitress is required to do several things such as arrive promptly to the table, suggest items (appetizer and salad bar), tell us how long it will take for our pizza to come out, and, of course, be friendly. While waiting for our food, we would note if the restaurant was clean, if tables were being bused, if the temperature was comfortable, if music was playing, if the bathrooms were clean, if employees were working hard or just sitting around, and anything else we might notice. When the food came out we would check to make sure it looked appetizing, had the right amount of topping distribution, was hot and cooked right, and note how long it took to get to the table. This information was put into a report form. Each Pizza Hut restaurant used this form and the scoring was based on 0–100 points. We faxed the reports over to the owner of the company and they were distributed to the district and store managers. Everyone discussed the reports, both good and bad. Employees who received good reports were rewarded and those with bad ones were retrained to make sure that whatever problems did occur were not repeated. No one at the restaurants ever knew who the individual shoppers were, including the Pizza Hut owner, so the reports would always remain objective. That's part of the beauty of mystery shopping. If the Pizza Hut owner went into one of his restaurants to do what we did, he would immediately be recognized and treated differently than the average customer. You can mystery shop just about any kind of business, such as supermarkets, restaurants and bars, car dealerships, travel agencies, malls, bookstores, etc. This book will not have many mystery shopping examples, but at least now you will know what I'm talking about.

I was getting married in May of 1996 (at age twenty-five) so I figured I would keep my full time job until then, save some money, and start the company part time. During the time before my wedding, I did not have much success getting clients. All I had ever really done was work at A&P and I didn't know anything about "the business world." I was only able to get one client, the aforementioned Pizza Hut. The owner had eighteen restaurants, so it was a start. During one of our first conversations he had asked me on the phone if I could fax him some information. I did not own a fax machine at the time and I said I couldn't. He assumed the machine was broken and accepted it at that. I quickly suggested that we get together and he invited me down for a meeting. I took a brochure with me that was embarrassing at best. Looking back, I wouldn't have even handed it in for a college class assignment, but at the time it was all I had. He must have seen something in me because he hired us, with no other clients, and we worked with them for over two years until his company was sold.

When May came, I took my two-week vacation for my honeymoon and never went back to A&P. I never gave them any notice or even told anyone I was leaving. When my final night was over, I just punched out and never went back. My father thought I was crazy to leave a job after nine years and give no notice with a new wife and a mortgage. What I wanted was to make it so that A&P would never hire me back. I did not want a safety net or something to fall back on. I had only one choice and that was to be successful. I also give a lot of credit to my wife. She supported me one hundred percent and has always had complete faith in me. I knew it was either now or never. A friend once said, "You can't steal second base if one foot is still on first."

The first few months were very hard. We got nowhere. I was petrified to make cold calls and I did nothing to sell our service. I had no friends in business that could help me or give me support. Some days, while my wife was at her job, I would just hide in bed under the sheets thinking how scared I was. I wound up taking a job delivering newspapers at three in the morning to bring in some extra money. Things were not looking bright. But I didn't quit and we didn't give up faith. Out of nowhere we got a call from a supermarket chain looking to try mystery shopping. They had called several other mystery shopping companies and none of them met with their satisfaction. I told their representative that I would have an evaluation form over to them the next day for her to look at. Having worked in the business for nine years I knew exactly what to look for. I copied the format of the Pizza Hut form with appropriate supermarket questions and faxed it over. The next day we were hired. During the same week I also got a call back from a bagel chain that I had gotten up the nerve to approach. I had figured that the meeting went nowhere, but now we had two new clients and were on our way. At least I was able to quit my paper route.

Over the next year and a half, we slowly gathered more and more clients. Our next big break came when we were featured in an article about mystery shopping on the front page of *The New York Times* business section in February of 1998. It pays to do PR. That article not only helped propel us out of our home office but also into other articles in *Vogue, Business Start-Ups,* and most of the major area newspapers. In 1998 I was included in two New Jersey publications, "40 Under 40" lists which highlighted up-and-coming people under the age of 40. In February of 1999, I was again in the *Times,* this time in a half page personality piece just about me. The business was growing and we were starting to get noticed.

But all was not perfect. My wife had quit her job and joined the company full time. The long hours and fights (better than Tyson/Holyfield) were taking their toll. It is very difficult to start a business with a spouse. Eventually, my wife wanted out of the business to start a family. I was tired of fighting and wanted to move on to other projects that I did not have the time to pursue. I, too, was ready to start a family. In January of 1999 my wife learned she was pregnant with our first child. After much discussion, we decided to sell the business. That June, I officially sold C&S Mystery Shoppers, Inc.

This book wound up turning into an unexpected entrepreneurial venture. I originally started out like most authors by writing query letters to agents (introduction letters about you and your book) and a book proposal (your ideas for the book, who it's marketed to, etc.). After several months of getting nowhere courting agents, I started to get discouraged. I did have several agents interested, but not quite ready to sign on the dotted line to represent me. One day I spoke to two of the agents that were interested. One wanted me to go in a different direction than I wanted to take the book, the other agent had not read my revised proposal and said she would get back to me. Both my wife and I were disappointed that all our hard work might be for nothing. One problem with book publishing today is that the market is so competitive that agents and publishers want books that they don't have to work hard to sell. A well-known author with an inferior book is often easier for agents and publishers to sell than an unknown author with a great book. It also takes most books a year to reach the shelves once the publisher has purchased them.

Then a light bulb went off in my head. I'm an entrepreneur, I wrote a book about entrepreneurship, why don't I publish the book mysef? I wrote a quality book that several agents have taken interest in. I had already written the proposal and come up with a marketing plan that the agent would use to sell the book to a publisher. Even after a book is printed, authors have to do their own promotion. I thought, if I'm already doing most of the work, why should I split the profits with a publisher and then have to pay an agent fifteen percent? If I publish the book myself, I wouldn't have to rewrite ideas to please an editor and I could have the book printed on my timetable. I was taking all the financial risks, but I would reap all the benefits. Isn't that a large part of what being an entrepreneur is?

That is how the introduction ended in the first edition. Since then I have embarked on a speaking career where I give workshops and seminars on goal setting/time management, customer service, and how to start a business. I have worked with companies such as Volvo, Wendy's, BellSouth, Yellow Book USA, and ShopRite. My self-publishing gamble also paid off. An editor at Thomson read my book and said, "We want to publish this book!" and that is what you hold in your hands.

So that is my story to date. I didn't read it in a textbook. I lived it firsthand. I hope some of the lessons I learned will make it easier for you to start your own company. Remember it all starts with a dream. . . .

"The quality of a man's life is in direct proportion to his commitment to excellence no matter what his chosen field of endeavor."—Vince Lombardi

MACHIAVELLIAN THOUGHTS

The business world is a cold place. You won't find any "touched by an angel" fuzziness or new age babble. It's hostile takeovers. It's pink slips. It's downsizing. Why does Bill Gates, chairman of one of the richest corporations in America, act like Microsoft is always under siege? Because it is. He knows that somewhere, maybe graduating from college or still just in the second grade, there is a younger, hungrier, more ambitious future "Bill Gates" ready to create his own Microsoft. Why are books like The Art of War, Leadership Secrets of Attila the Hun, *and* How to Swim With the Sharks and Not Get Eaten Alive *popular with business people? Because it is a jungle out there.*

Do You Have the
Right Stuff?

"The critical ingredient is getting off your butt and doing something. It's as simple as that. A lot of people have ideas, but there are few who decide to do something about them now. Not tomorrow. Not next week. But today. The true entrepreneur is a doer, not a dreamer." —**Founder of Atari**

As you can imagine, I meet a lot of people that want to start their own business. They have wonderful ideas and are full of excitement, but sometimes they need to temper that with a dose of reality. Many people have no idea what it takes to start a successful business. They see business people who started a business fifteen years ago who make great incomes, drive luxury cars, live in nice houses, and think that that could be them, too. What they don't usually see is the sweat equity that business owners put in to reach that point. They have no idea of just how hard you have to work to make a profit and sustain it. Business owners *can* make lots of money, but it is usually after years of building a business. That being said, it's still a great life, as long as you know what you're in for.

I teach a workshop on starting your own business and I start off by asking several questions to see if the would-be-entrepreneurs have really thought it through. The first point I make is that there is no "typical entrepreneur." Business owners come from every background you could imagine. Fred W. Smith, the founder of Federal Express, was a graduate of Yale and used $4 million of his family's money to start the business. Conversely, Andrew Carnegie never made it past the third grade, yet went on to become the richest man in America. (He was richer in his day than Bill Gates is today.) Tom Monaghan, founder of Domino's Pizza, grew up in an orphanage. Going to an Ivy League school and getting an MBA will not guarantee success and starting from behind the pack does not mean you have to stay there. This is, after all, the land of opportunity.

I believe that most of the qualities that make up a successful entrepreneur are intangible. I know that some organizations have tried to come up with tests to determine who would make a good entrepreneur, but how do you test for heart? Determination? Vision? Faith? Persistence?

During my workshop I use my brother and myself to illustrate the point that some people are entrepreneurs and some are not. I love my brother very much and we are very close. Early on, after my first business had achieved some success, I made an offer to my brother: Anytime he wanted to, he could quit his job and come work with me. I was going to give him half the business. Of course, we love and trust each other. I figured we could work together to build something great. On paper, my brother had everything; he kicked my butt on the SAT, graduated with honors from the Rutgers University School of Business, and worked in the headquarters of a multibillion-dollar company. (I didn't have the grades to get into the business school, which reminds me of a quote I've often heard, "The world is run by 'C' students.") One day I got the call. My brother was ready to join me. And he did . . . for about a week. Then I was given my notice and he got his old job back. He is a bright guy, but he just doesn't make a good entrepreneur. For all the questions I will bring up in this chapter, he would answer "No," while I would answer "Yes." Before you invest your life savings and quit your day job, ask yourself, "Am I more like Mark, the entrepreneurial type, or am I more like Scott, the corporate type?"

ARE YOU A SELF-STARTER?

Being your own boss is a double-edged sword. On one hand, you follow your dreams and visions for where the company should go. You make the decisions and give the orders. On the other hand, there is no one there telling you that you have to get something done. There is no one there advising you. I would often work seven days a week for weeks straight. There was no one telling me that I had to work twenty hours this weekend to get a project done. *I* had to set that alarm to get up at six on Sunday and get myself to work. Every job has some aspect of it that you won't care for. When you're in charge, it's up to you to still do the things you don't like to do to get the job done. There won't be anyone looking over your shoulder to hold you accountable. That first morning I asked my brother to come over to my house about 6:00 AM. He showed up not too happy at about 7:30 AM. It was downhill from there.

CAN YOU GO SIX MONTHS TO TWO YEARS WITHOUT GETTING PAID?

Obviously, you go into business to make money. For most new businesses those dollars go right back into the business and not into the owner's bank account. Many people don't realize that in start-up ventures, most entrepreneurs don't draw any salary. They take money out of their bank account. Sometimes, a spouse will financially support them. It's rare for them to draw a bank check of any amount, and if they do, it's years away from the salary they were used to getting paid. There are often up-front costs that have to be paid first. Let's say the business is successful and now you need more inventory. You're going to use your cash flow to pay for it. You might need employees and believe it or not they'll expect to get paid every week no matter how things are going. Of course there are the fixed costs. The phone company likes to get paid monthly. It's always a good idea to pay your rent. The truth is, you're the last one to see any of the money, if there is any left at the end of the month. Just because your business is growing, doesn't mean it's making a profit or has a positive cash flow. This obviously doesn't go on forever but realize that in the beginning you're the last one to get paid and that you will need money to personally live off of for up to a year or two. The entrepreneur will forgo some paychecks for the greater benefits down the road. Other people like the security that every Thursday "X" amount will be directly deposited into the checking account.

ARE YOU WILLING TO GIVE UP VACATIONS, EVENINGS, AND WEEKENDS?

When I owned my first company, if you had mentioned the word vacation to me, I would have had to look it up in the dictionary. My brother gets three weeks vacation and five sick days. I would take the third Wednesday of the month off and wonder, "What am I going to do with a whole day?" This might sound ridiculous to you if you are used to having every weekend off, but that's life as an entrepreneur. A movie with my wife on Thursday night? What's that? Can we stop over at 1:00 PM on Saturday for lunch? Are you kidding, in the middle of the workday? I'm not exaggerating in this section. Starting a business is like having two full-time jobs. Of course, it does get better over time. I'll sum it up with this example: I wanted to take my wife to see a Broadway play, so I ordered tickets six months in advance to be sure that we would both have that day off.

ARE YOU A DECISION MAKER?

As an entrepreneur you are always making decisions, both large and small. It just goes with the job of being in charge. You can't be the type that fears making the wrong decision or needs to evaluate all the information before deciding. As you read this book you'll learn of the many mistakes I've made, so don't be afraid that one or two mistakes will ruin everything. I've made mistakes in every aspect of my professional career, but I'm still around. You can't afford to wait until you have all of the information, because you will **never** have all the information. You have to make decisions with the best available information and live with it. One of the biggest mistakes people make is to delay a decision until the last possible moment. Often, if you make a decision early and it turns out to be the wrong one, there's still time to fix it. If you've delayed making a decision until you absolutely have to, then you're often stuck. Highlight these next couple of lines with your marker. You will make mistakes. Everyone does. Entrepreneurs brighter than us will make them, too. I've included a whole chapter on learning from mistakes. The only people that don't make mistakes are the ones who don't risk, don't take chances, who don't say, "What if we did this or tried that?" In other words, people unwilling to take risks live very boring lives and never accomplish anything.

ARE YOU A PEOPLE PERSON?

I'll only touch on the topic here, because I also cover it in a later chapter, but everything we do involves people. Obvious enough—right? But if you are someone who prefers being left alone or would rather stay in your circle of friends, you might not want to choose entrepreneurship as a career. It's not enough to be pleasant around people, but you really need to master the art of *Winning Friends and Influencing People* (a book I'll talk about later). Think about all the relationships that you'll need to foster: customers, competitors, vendors, bankers, and prospects, not to mention your family when you're convincing them that all the time you spend working is worth it.

DO YOU HANDLE REJECTION WELL?

No one likes rejection, but it's a part of business. I feel that if I don't hear a "No" somewhere in my day, then I'm not doing enough prospecting. For some people, it's a hard concept to deal with that not everyone will love your product. I know that not everyone who attends my seminars will think I'm the greatest thing since sliced bread. You can't please everyone. If I worry about the one person in the third row who is bored I'm going to lose sight of the ten people that are enjoying the seminar and learning from it. A seminar attendee I was speaking to one day clearly illustrated that if you can't handle rejection, you shouldn't go into business for yourself. She told me that her mother had wanted the two of them to go into business together to start a bakery. She said the only thing that has stopped her mother was that several years ago someone criticized one of her cakes at a church function. That one rejection has held her back for years! I told the person that I thought she answered her own question about going into business with her mom. Did her mother think that a customer would never complain? What would happen the first time a banker said "No" to their loan application? In the end, the mother is much better off talking about starting a business than ever doing it.

DO YOU THINK WELL ON YOUR FEET?

This also ties in with decision making. In the beginning of my first company, I was often asked questions that I had never thought of before. They were usually requests from customers or prospects that I hadn't been asked yet or hadn't anticipated. I often had to make a split second decision—could we or couldn't we fulfill the request—then give a convincing answer. By years three and four I had heard all the requests and had answers for them. In the beginning, you're often feeling your way around, learning the ropes yourself, but you can't tell that to a client or prospect. They expect that you've thought it out already. You can't say, "Wow, I've never thought of that. Give me a week and I'll get back to you." I've read countless stories of entrepreneurs who seized opportunities because they could think well on their feet. I'll share one of mine with you. After reading about us in *The New York Times,* a reporter from *Vogue* called our office. My wife answered the call and it was explained to her that they wanted to do a story on mystery shopping. My wife couldn't figure out how we could work with a fashion magazine and politely turned her down. Meanwhile, she gave the reporter the names of several other mystery shopping companies to call. She also never told me *Vogue* had called. About a week later, not being able to find anyone to do the story with, the reporter called back. My wife handed me the phone and briefed me, "Reporter on phone from *Vogue.* They want to do a story. I said 'No,' but they couldn't find anyone else." I had the same amount of time to react as my wife, and we wound up getting a two-page story. My ability to think on my feet and make a quick decision is what got the story written.

DO YOU LIKE TO SELL?

When most people think of selling, they think of used car dealers and snake oil salesmen. Most mothers want their kids to grow up to be doctors, lawyers, or architects; how many say, "Go be a salesperson?" Too bad. Selling is a skilled profession, and your ability to sell could catapult you to higher levels in life. Whether you realize it or not, we're always selling. Some just do it better than others. If you have been pulled over by a police officer, do you just say, "Thanks for the ticket" or would you try to talk your way out of it? That's selling. If you've asked someone to marry you, and you explained why they should spend the rest of their life with you, that's selling. If you've ever been in a meeting and you are trying to convince everyone else why your plan is the best, that's selling. If you can see how important selling is in these daily life scenarios, think what it means to your business when you are selling customers on why your product or service is the best, bankers on why they should lend you money, employees on why they should work for a start-up company, and vendors on why they should extend you credit. Selling is everywhere.

DO YOU HANDLE CRISES WELL?

With a start-up company it seems like it's always something that goes wrong. This machine breaks. That delivery is late. Those packages got switched. Sometimes everything is fine, and the customer is still upset. No matter how well you plan, unexpected things happen. If you can't handle working on at least one crisis everyday, don't be an entrepreneur. You really have to roll with the punches. This is true even in established companies. Before my wife worked for me, she worked for an office supply company. While working there, one of their drivers was taking a delivery from New Jersey to Massachusetts and got pulled over. Because his truck log was not properly filled out and they would not let him back on the road, the owner of the company had to drive to Massachusetts to get him. He had owned the business for twenty years and was at least a millionaire, but that's all a part of owning a business.

WOULD YOU BE ABLE TO FIRE SOMEONE?

Could you do it? It's probably one of the worst, if not the worst, responsibility that a business owner has. Could you let someone go that you've worked with for a year and you know has two young kids, but they're just not doing their job? I have seen companies where bad employees affected the workplace like a cancer simply because no one had the guts to say, "You're fired."

DO YOU WANT TOTAL RESPONSIBILITY
AND ACCOUNTABILITY?

When you start a business, you're it. If there is a question that can't be answered, people turn to you. If the company is having problems focusing, you're the one at the helm. If you are having trouble making payroll, you'd better find some money. If someone breaks into the building at 3:00 AM, you're there to fill out the police report in your bathrobe.

You need many of the previously-mentioned traits to be successful at any job, but not to the extent you would need them as an entrepreneur. Yes, my brother has responsibility and has to make decisions, but he also has a boss that makes the larger decisions for him. He won't be asked to fire someone. He doesn't have total responsibility and accountability. If he has a bad month, his company will still be around. Some people are better at running a business, and some are better at being employees. I know that I would have trouble working in a corporate setting.

I don't want to paint a totally bleak picture of your entrepreneurial future. There are tremendous rewards to being an entrepreneur. I'm a self-starter, and I love being able to set my own pace instead of being confined in an organization. You will be swelling with pride as you watch your idea go from a concept to a business. I also love the challenge of not knowing what's around the corner or where my business will take me. But, like everything, it has its downside. If you weren't able to say "Yes" to all or at least most of the questions asked earlier, you shouldn't start your own business. You have to give a tremendous amount of yourself. I am constantly thinking about my business—the other books I want to write, mentally practicing my workshops in my head. As a matter of fact, I thought of the outline for this section when I was lying in bed; my 2-year-old couldn't sleep so my wife brought her into our room, and as she tossed, turned, drank her juice, and babbled to us, I came up with the idea for this chapter. I was thinking two things: (1) I wish this kid would go to sleep, and, (2) I hope I remember all of this in the morning.

POINT TO PONDER

- I think after the Internet bust, many people's business expectations came back to reality. Too many people had dollar signs in their eyes without having any idea of what running a business actually required. There is a basic principle that goes back to the Bible, "As you sow, so shall you reap." You don't get something for nothing in this life. There are no shortcuts to success. All the successful entrepreneurs you know sowed first and reaped later.

2

Watch Out for Number One—Part 1

"Trust no one." —**Deep Throat to agent Scully, in the** *X-Files*

"The most striking contradiction of our civilization is the fundamental reverence for truth which we profess and thoroughgoing disregard for it which we practice." —**Vilhjalmur Stefansson**

I don't want to be cynical, but I can't help it. I want to have faith in mankind, but I haven't seen that much to be hopeful about. In business, it's, "Watch out for number one." Forget all that warm, fuzzy, new-age stuff you see on talk shows. At the end of the day, no one really cares about you. If you're truthful, you'll probably admit that you don't really care what happens to the people that you meet, either. That salesperson in your office might have been very nice and genuinely interested in helping your company, but if someone else can offer the same service at half the price, are you really going to lose any sleep over not choosing his company? No. Do you want to see your co-worker get fired? No. But if they do, will you lend them money and offer to let them stay at your house until they're back on their feet? Probably not.

I'm not trying to imply that one has to be ruthless or unfeeling to get ahead. But let's face it, there are certain instincts that we all have, including the survival instinct. I have a wife and child, and my concern is putting a roof over their heads and food in their mouths. You undoubtedly have the same feelings about protecting your own family.

Niccolo Machiavelli knew this when he wrote *The Prince.* Times and circumstances have changed since the book was written, but people haven't. Machiavelli lived between 1469 and 1527 in Florence, Italy. He held public office and wrote several books. He acquired a reputation for advocating a ruthless, scientific approach to politics. His ideas were resurrected by the Romantics of the nineteenth century. They argued that his works had a moral base: the belief that excesses of cruelty and dishonesty can be justified in the interests of patriotism. In *The Prince*, Machiavelli tries to show the title character that evil is unavoidable in all human activity, how to recognize this, and use it to his advantage. The book deals with politics, but the ideas can be applied to business, as is evidenced by the 1998 book, *The New Machiavelli: The Art of Politics in Business.* Machiavelli understood the capacity of evil that lurks in everyone. The business people I have met have not been evil, but they do know who they are watching out for, and it's not me.

I don't believe people do most things without having some ulterior motive. Even good deeds usually aren't done without ulterior motives, although we may want to fool ourselves into believing otherwise. I will admit why I do things. I speak at colleges for free because I want to refine my speaking style and get better at being in front of an audience. That's not to say I don't do my best and hope that the students learn valuable information. I'm just not doing it totally out of the kindness of my heart. I will often help someone and ask for nothing in return. What I get is a good feeling about myself. It strokes my ego. When I go into a meeting, I try to figure out if the person sitting across from me has an ulterior motive in mind. Am I just there as a ploy to get their current supplier to lower their price? Is that person getting three proposals to show their boss how busy they are to justify their job? Am I supplying them with free information? Or do they genuinely need my service? I shake hands with my right hand and look for the proverbial sword in their left. You can imagine my surprise when I first came across business people that fit into the above categories. It was all a part of my initiation into the business world.

People are not always what they appear to be. I would much rather have someone walk up to me and tell me they're going to try to woo my clients away rather than being covert or underhanded like the fox waiting in the woods. I first ran across this type at a mystery shopping convention. This woman owned one of the more established companies and was a keynote speaker. She spoke about all the trials and tribulations she had when she started out. Her speaking sounded intelligent, but I just couldn't believe her story. Anybody that incompetent would have been out of business in six months. I don't know if anyone else felt it, but I believed she was trying to get everyone to lower their guard to her. Her company was one of the bigger ones there and not one to be taken lightly. What better way to play the "Little ol' me" role than in front of all your competitors? To me, she seemed very phony and manipulative. This was the first mystery shopping convention ever, and she was on many of the committees to establish ground rules and objectives for the association. I'm sure her sly-as-a-fox abilities helped her. One thing under discussion was who should be allowed to join the association, and one idea she brought up was that membership should be allowed only to companies that had been around a certain number of years. Since mystery shopping is a fairly new, growing industry, that didn't leave many companies eligible, but it would have certainly included her company.

Often, people are deceitful and underhanded because they're out to get everything they can. Of course we're all out to get the largest piece of the pie for ourselves, but these guys will take every last crumb and the plate, too. I met this type up close when I went to sell my business. Another mystery shopping company owner came to look at my business. He was all business and lacked most of the people skills that we are always told are so important. He tried a little bit of "that bonding stuff," but it didn't seem natural. I tried to joke with him, but my jokes fell like rocks being thrown off a bridge. He just wanted facts and figures and how my clients could be worked into his company. Luckily, I had a business acquaintance on my side in the meeting to help me along so I didn't make a mistake. Even after the meeting, when we went to get something to eat, he just barraged me with more questions. I did not get a good feeling from him after the meeting, and when he e-mailed his offer I knew why. I read it and wondered, "What do I get?" He would get my clients; I would get health insurance (which I already had), a chance to work for him on commission, and a couple of intangibles that did not amount to much. If I could live with those terms, we'd have a deal. Had it been the twelfth century, he would have taken my wife, killed my pigs, and made me an indentured servant. For further examples, rent the movie *Wall Street* or *Barbarians at the Gate.*

Others will use you for what they need and then throw you out like stale bread. They're nice and friendly and appear supportive as long as you're giving them what they need: free advice, information, and an inexpensive service. Try to get some help out of them, though, and they act as if they've never heard of you. After they get all the free advice they need on a new project, you disappear from their Rolodex.

Remember, it's okay to watch out for yourself in business. You can do it and still go to heaven. I'm just trying to make you aware. There are those out there with more experience, more resources, more greed, and they will run over you if you're not careful. I'm not a pessimist; I'm a huge optimist. I'm just trying to call it like it is, so you can be on your guard. Hopefully you won't have to deal with the type of people I described, but more than likely you will run into them, so be forewarned. Don't think that I am being overly dramatic. *It is a jungle out there.*

I don't want you going out there totally paranoid, but I just want you to keep your eyes open and be alert. People and companies will do whatever is necessary and legal (and sometimes illegal) to help gain the advantage. A good example came from the cover story in *USA Today* (August 9, 1999), "The New P.I. Gumshoes Do Their Snooping on the Internet." The gist of the article is that with technology, there is nothing that "they" can't find out about you. The bottom line is that information is power. The more information a company has on a competitor or its employees the more power they have. Some examples of companies that hire private investigators are American Airlines, Boeing, State Farm Insurance, Lloyds of London, and Reebok. Hopefully a competitor of yours will never want access to your social security number, home address, unlisted phone number, property you own, other businesses you're involved in, credit report, or bank account balances. It is important to go out there and see things as they really are. You might think "the spy game" only happens in the movies, but the *USA Today* article listed just a few of the major companies that employ private investigators. Do you wonder what your employer does?

"The power of accurate observation is commonly called cynicism by those who have not got it."—George Bernard Shaw

POINT TO PONDER

- Don't be afraid to keep *your* company's best interests in mind. You are not being ruthless, just smart.

2

Watch Out for Number One—Part 2

I liked having my own company and not just because of the obvious reasons, such as being my own boss or the potential money I could make. I enjoyed the roller coaster ride that is the essence of being an entrepreneur. When I first started out as an entrepreneur, I was like the young naïve hero in the movies. I was blissfully unaware of the "evil" forces "out there." As the movie unfolds, the hero is exposed to these elements, becomes more aware of his surroundings, and must adapt to them while keeping his virtues and ideals. While writing the chapter "Watch Out for Number One" I wondered if I was exaggerating a bit to make my point. I decided to do a little experiment. I would read my local paper, *The Star Ledger,* for two weeks and see if I saw any evidence to back up my claim. Unfortunately, just about every day I was cutting out an article about the underside of business. Here are a few examples:

- *Vitamin firms hit with big fines in Canada.* "Five international pharmaceutical companies were slapped with a C$88.4 million fine Wednesday by a Canadian court over a global vitamin price fixing conspiracy."
- *State to hear evidence in Bally's 'payoff' probe.* "At the heart of the hearing before the state Casino Control Commission (Florida) is a 62-page report by the Division of Gaming Enforcement focusing on $240,000 Bally's Entertainment paid in consulting fees to Bo Johnson, the former Assembly Speaker in Florida. Johnson was ultimately convicted of tax evasion for not reporting $1.6 million in consulting fees he accepted from Bally's over six years." The report also discusses allegations that Bally's chairman was aware of the payment.
- *Schering donation raises eyebrows on patent bill.* "On May 26, the Democratic Senatorial Campaign Committee held a fund raiser in Newark and collected a $50,000 contribution from drug maker Schering-Plough. The next day in Washington, Sen. Robert Toricelli (D-NJ), chairman of the campaign committee,

introduced legislation that could mean billions of dollars to Schering-Plough by permitting a three year patent extension for Claritin®, it's blockbuster allergy medicine."

- *Prosecutors: Financier tried an end run.* "Martin A. Armstrong Jr., the financial guru accused of bilking Japanese investors out of about $1 billion, may have tried to thwart U.S. prosecutors by trying to liquidate his New Jersey company in a West Indies island court."

- *Cheap car parts at a high cost.* "(Marion, IL) A jury ordered State Farm to pay $456 million to 4.7 million customers yesterday in a lawsuit accusing the nation's largest car insurer of using inferior parts for auto body repairs. The plaintiffs still are seeking an additional $4 billion on their claim that State Farm deliberately deceived customers about the quality of the parts."

While my wife was reading my first draft, she questioned if I was making too big of a deal about this one point. *I feel this is the most important lesson I learned during the years I ran my own company.* I can't stress too much how true the "Watch Out for Number One" idea is. In the above examples, there are large multimillion-dollar companies involved in price fixing, payoffs, fraud, etc. Don't think that one of these companies would think twice about trying to crush a young up-start. Who do you think they're watching out for?

3

Show Me the Money!

*"When a fellow says, 'It ain't the money but the principle of the thing,'
it's the money."* —**Frank McKinney Hubbard**

"When it is a question of money, everybody is of the same religion."
—**Voltaire**

When Rod Tidwell (Cuba Gooding Jr.) told his agent Jerry
Maguire (Tom Cruise) in the movie of the same name, "Show
me the money," he had it exactly right. It all comes down to
money. Everyone is a friend until you start talking dollars and
cents. Then it's business. Obviously, unless your business is non-
profit, the goal of any company is to make the most money it
can. If you charge a dollar for an item and you find a way to get
$1.25 for it, you'll take it.

I am sometimes asked if I think that it matters in making it in
the business world if someone is a minority, a woman, young,
old, etc. I don't think those factors matter that much. There is
racism, sexism, and prejudice in the business world, but unfortunately that exists everywhere in the world and probably always
will. A female businessperson or a nineteen-year-old entrepreneur might have to work harder to be taken seriously or get the
attention of others, but I believe if they have a workable, money-
making idea, they will be able to move ahead. In the end, the
only color that counts is green. The old greenback quickly has
a way of helping people put aside their prejudices.

Unfortunately, in this highly competitive society of ours, it all
comes down to money. Loyalty is just a concept in movies. When
the CEO of a large company announces 10,000 layoffs, what
happens? The company's stock price goes up. Why? Because he
is cost cutting and streamlining. He is going to set the company
back on track. What about the 10,000 workers and their fami-
lies? No one thinks about them. My company had a client we
worked very hard for, for over a year. We did shops in their stores
every week and did a good job. One day we got a "To whom it

may concern" letter asking us to cancel the service—no reason given—basically, "It's been nice knowing you." You are always at the mercy of someone with a pen that wants to cut the budget. It's no different if you decide to open a retail business. Someone sells the same item down the street for ten percent less, and no matter how long your customers have been coming to your store, you still have to worry that some will leave.

I have made a conscious attempt to not let money become my master, but you have to walk a fine line. If you have a big heart and small bank account, you might not be in business long.

As a new entrepreneur, you'll have to fight the urge that you want to see the money immediately. In society today, we want instant gratification. When I see a 26-year-old worth $250 million after dot.comming his business, I sometimes think, "Why I am bothering with my line of business?" but the twenty-something zillionare is the exception rather than the rule. If you build an enduring business, whether it is a record store, restaurant, or dot.com, in time, you will see the money.

POINT TO PONDER

- Here are two examples to show you that you can be socially conscious *and* still succeed in business: Ben & Jerry's and Newman's Own. In 1985, the Ben & Jerry's Foundation was established. Ben & Jerry's makes a donation, at its board's discretion, of approximately seven-and-a-half percent of its pre-tax profits. Newman's Own was established in 1982 by actor Paul Newman and in 1999 it passed the $100 million mark in total donations. Paul Newman donates one hundred percent of his after-tax profits from the sale of Newman's Own products for education and charitable purposes. Way to go "Cool Hand Luke"!

4

Let's Face It:
People Lie to You

"Ask any woman her age and nine times out of ten she'll guess wrong."
—Bob Murphy, humorist

"I have nothing to hide. The White House has nothing to hide."
—Richard Nixon

"I did not have sexual relations with that woman." **—Bill Clinton**

I was very naïve when I went into business and it was probably the reason I learned so much. My mom taught me to always tell the truth, and I was usually very good about it. So when I got into business it's how I figured everyone would be, with the exception of a couple of rotten apples. I thought, just like George Washington, everybody tells the truth. Well, I quickly learned otherwise.

For example, when I first followed up on sales letters, rarely would anyone say they weren't interested. They would say, "I haven't had time to look at it yet," "I have to ask my partner," or "I can't authorize anything." So I would persist and call them back another day. If I was lucky enough to get through, I would get the old, "I still haven't had a chance to look at it," even though they had probably thrown it out long ago.

Say I want to call Ms. Smith and the secretary asks, "Who's calling?" When I reply, "Mark Csordos" and she'll respond, "She's not in." I always think, don't you know she's not in before you ask my name? Of course, they're screening her calls and I'm not on the 'A' list. At least not yet, anyway.

Sometimes people lie to you because they're too nice and don't want to hurt your feelings. They'd rather say something vague and hope you go away on your own, than say, "No." They might think they are doing you a favor by sparing your feelings, but you can waste a lot of time on this type of prospect.

Be honest, we've all screened our calls or told a salesperson that you still wanted to think about it when you knew you weren't going to buy from them. However, there are lies that can really cost your company a lot of time and money.

Some companies have no intention of using your services or buying your products, they just want what you know for free. For example, a restaurant chain could call me up and say they are thinking about beginning a mystery shopping program. They could have no intention of using an outside firm, but they need to know how to do it so they could do it in-house. They invite me in and ask for sample copies of our forms and procedures. Then during the meeting I will explain to them how to run a program, where I find our shoppers, what to look for, etc. They say it was a great meeting and that they'll think about it. Meanwhile, they take my presentation and start to build their own program. But they don't have it all quite right and still have a couple of questions. Could I come in for another meeting? Sure. I answer their questions in the second meeting and they say they'll make a decision soon. I follow up in two weeks and I'm told that they've decided not to do the project after all, but they thank me for my time and tell me they'll keep me on file (if they ever need more free information). This happens all the time. A friend of mine called it "unpaid consulting." Other times a company can use you as leverage to get concessions from their current supplier. Sometimes it's unavoidable. You have to have some faith in people and you won't know until it's over that you've been duped. But, the more experience you gain, the sooner you will realize when this is happening. After a while you get a feel for dealing with customers and clients. The chapter titled "Listen, Listen, Listen" will also help. The more questions you ask the customer, the more you can sort out their true needs.

Deception is a part of the game and I am guilty of it, too. I used to have my friend call up competing mystery shopping companies and pretend to be a company owner wanting mystery shopping information. He would have the information sent to his house "so his employees wouldn't find out." Is that wrong? Yes, but they wouldn't have given me the information if I asked and business is a matter of survival. I do think if they had asked more probing questions, like I recommend, they could have possibly weeded my friend out. I'm sure I've been victimized that way, too. I remember a person saying they read about us in a magazine while on an airplane to visit some friends. They asked if I could send information to their friend's fax number (with whom they were staying). They gave me no other number or address to reach them. Of course I rushed to get the information out and, of course, I never heard from them again.

Here is another example to reinforce this point. After I had been in business for a couple of years, I read a magazine article about mystery shopping. At the end, it gave the readers the address of one of the larger mystery shopping companies where people interested in starting a company of this type could write with their questions. I wrote a letter to see what type of information I would receive back. I received a form letter stating that, because of the number of requests for information they had received, they could not answer each one individually. The letter gave some very basic information on starting a company. When I first read the letter, I got a laugh out of it. First, I realized they never had any intention of answering any questions. This was a way for them to see how many people had an interest in starting a mystery shopping company (future competitors). Second, the letter was meant to deter people from starting a company. It was laughable. I remember the letter stating that someone would need between $50,000–$100,000 to start a mystery shopping company. This was totally untrue. I was already making a profit with my company and we only had about $2,500 in start-up capital. The letter also told about all the struggles that the company had experienced just to reach the modest point they were at. I hope their letter did not deter people from venturing into mystery shopping. It actually had the reverse effect on me. I figured if this company was trying this hard to keep competitors away, there must be something to this "mystery shopping." I guess this experience was a good lesson in both "Let's Face It: People Lie to You" and "Watch Out for Number One."

The next level of lying, far up the ladder, is the "burn-in-hell" lies. I still have a clear conscience for having my friend pretend to be a business owner and ask for information. I never used the information to steal away clients; I just wanted to know how advanced other companies were and what they charged, since there is so little information available on mystery shopping as an industry. I include the burn-in-hell lies to show that sometimes it isn't just an occasional bad apple or questionable judgment by individuals. These are lies perpetrated on a large scale to the detriment of others. I'll go back to the examples in "Watch Out for Number One—Part 2." Five executives from international pharmaceutical companies agreed on global vitamin price fixing. A well-known company like Bally's was involved in a "payoff" probe. State Farm was ordered by a jury to pay $456 million in a lawsuit accusing them of using inferior parts for auto body repairs. Was State Farm completely honest with their policyholders? The jury did not think so. I've saved the coup de gras for last—Big Tobacco. This is an industry so bad that I went to the library and found *entire books* on tobacco litigation. It's amazing how any tobacco executive can sleep at night, but then again billions of dollars in profits over the decades can help ease the conscience. I just want to give you a little excerpt from a court case to show that some business people will look you in the eye and flat out lie to you. Some lies I've discussed are rather harmless, but ask anyone who has ever gotten sick from cigarettes about the effects of their lies. In the case, *Cippolone* v. *Liggett,* the President of Liggett, Kinsley & Dey was questioned about the tumors caused in the company's mouse painting experiments. (These were studies done by his company that found that the company's cigarettes caused tumors in mice and rabbits.) The plaintiff's lawyer asked why the company had done the experiments. The following exchange ensued.

> **Lawyer:** What was the purpose of this?
> **Dey:** To try to reduce tumors on the backs of mice.
> **Lawyer:** It had nothing to do with health and welfare of human beings? Is that correct?
> **Dey:** That's correct.
> **Lawyer:** How much did the study cost?
> **Dey:** A lot . . . Probably between $15 million or more.
> **Lawyer:** And this was to save rats, right? Or mice? You spent all this money to save mice the problem of developing tumors, is that correct?
> **Dey:** I have stated what we did. (*Smokescreen.* Philip J. Hilts, pg. 24)

What a guy! All that (the $15 million was in 1950's dollars) to save mice. It's good to know that the tobacco companies have a deep concern for mice. I just want you to be aware that the business world is a tough place and not everyone plays by the rules. While I was writing this book, Microsoft was in the midst of being sued by the government in an antitrust suit alleging unfair competitive practices. They're only watching out for their best interests.

Why all the lying? Don't these people have mothers? They lie because there are no repercussions, unless they're doing it to a grand jury. It's a part of business. A bad part, but nonetheless, a part.

POINT TO PONDER

- I'm not saying there aren't many good people in the business world as well as companies that care about their employees, their customers, and the impact they have on society. What I am saying is that there are deceptions everywhere, and you have to be on your guard. Companies have the instinct to survive just like individuals and many are going to do whatever it takes. It happens large and small. After all of the facts were known, do you think that State Farm's customers felt that they were being told the entire truth?

5

Don't Take It Personally

"The world is a comedy to those that think, a tragedy to those that feel."
—**Horace Walpole (1717-1797)**

"The advantage of having a hard heart is that it will take a lot to break it." —**W. Burton Baldry**

When I was just starting out, a business friend told me that everyone needs "ego strokes." Who doesn't like to be told they look nice, that they're funny, smart, caring, dependable, etc? The problem is that we're all "stroke deprived." What we usually get is, "Have you gained weight?" "Why wasn't that report done by Friday?" "Did you forget to . . . ?" So we all go out into the world looking to get "stroked," but it rarely happens. The business world is not where you get *your* emotional needs met. You have to call your mom for that.

I'm sure you've heard that one of the biggest fears people have about selling is dealing with rejection. The best advice I can give is to not take it personally. I realize that's harder to do then it sounds. If you want to survive, you must develop a thick skin. When you meet with a customer they will rarely flatter you. It's *your* job to make *them* feel good. What you hear is, "Your price is too high," "I actually like company XYZ better," or "Your service isn't that good." There is also the flat-out rejection, and it often comes without any good or apparent reason.

When I started, I had trouble with this. What I did, and what most people do, is *take the rejection personally.* My friend explained to me that *the customers don't know me.* What customers are rejecting is something about my service or company, which is independent of Mark Csordos, the person. The customers didn't know if I went to college or prison after high school. They didn't know if I was married, had kids, what my favorite baseball team was, or what my hopes and dreams were. They didn't know *me.* If they said, "No" they were turning down Mark the salesman and not Mark the person. It is a hard thing to separate, but you'll have to if you want to succeed and keep your sanity.

Everyone gets rejected and the more ambitious and successful you are, the more rejection you have to get used to. Anyone who is successful will have critics. Every president, no matter what he does for the country, gets criticized and often ridiculed in the papers and in the media.

In your business dealings get used to hearing, "What have you done for me lately?" Look at Wall Street. A company can be up 400% in a year, but if they come out with disappointing earnings, the stock will almost always go down. No one will coddle you in the business world. If Microsoft goes out of business, no one, except Microsoft employees, will cry for Bill Gates.

I looked up Disney stock online because it is one of the companies I follow for my personal investments. The company had a rough 1999, but for the most part they have been a Wall Street darling for the past decade, and Michael Eisner helped to turn the company around when they made him Chairman and CEO in 1984. I checked out a Disney message board, and Eisner and the management team were described by some as "idiots," "out of touch," and "they should be fired." The only thing most Disney shareholders want to know is, "What have you done for me lately?" When I went back to review this chapter several months later, Disney stock had rebounded nicely. A quick check on the stock's message board showed their management had magically smartened up.

I remember when one long-term client let us go. All we got was a form letter addressed "To whom it may concern," stating they wanted to drop the service. There was no explanation or anything, just an impersonal note. That moment opened my eyes in a sense. The years of working with the client and spending countless hours performing the shops and trying to help them to improve fell by the wayside. Once they decided that they no longer needed the service, we were out. It was as simple as that.

While trying to get this book published I was riddled with rejections. Over forty agents turned me down for one reason or another. One agent said she liked the idea, but thought the book was too philosophical. That same week another agent rejected me saying the book was too basic. How can it be both? There's the "form letter" rejection, the "material doesn't suit our needs" rejection, the "book doesn't meet our standards" rejection, and the "we're too busy to even reject you" rejection. If I had taken all those rejections personally, I wouldn't have been able to write out a grocery list.

A trick that might help separate you, the person, from you, the businessperson, is to think of yourself playing a role, like an actor. When you're at work, you are the businessperson. When you're at home, you are the spouse, the parent, the neighbor, etc. They are different roles and shouldn't overlap with each other. If you had a bad day in the "businessperson" role, it shouldn't affect your role as a parent. It's not always easy to separate the roles, but it can be done if you make a conscious effort to do so.

Another trick is to think of yourself as a castle surrounded by a moat. Nothing can get inside unless you let it in. If someone gives you something that could create bad feelings, don't lower the drawbridge and let it in. It's like the expression, "It will only bother you if you let it."

POINTS TO PONDER

- I've been rejected by agents and publishers, by colleges and businesses, and no one ever gave "I don't like you" as the reason.

- The loftier your goals, the more rejection you'll find on the way to achieving them.

6

Give Your Best, but Don't Give Your Soul

"Whatever I have tried to do in life, I have tried with my heart to do well." —**Charles Dickens**

I sometimes felt like I cared about my clients' results more than they did. I would find myself thinking about ways to improve their service, whether I was driving around, at the dinner table, or lying in bed. I would get very frustrated when I did not see improvement in their stores. After a while I realized that this type of worrying was useless. I was doing my best. If the clients didn't care enough about their own stores, *that was their problem.* I was paid to mystery shop their stores and occasionally meet with them to discuss the results and how to improve them. I believe we did our job very well. I was not paid to worry about their stores when I was having dinner or watching a movie with my wife.

This lesson hit me like a ton of bricks one day when I was meeting with the president of one of our oldest clients. His stores seemed to hit a wall when it came to making any improvement. I believe it was because of his management style. The managers did not like the mystery shopping because they would get chewed out over every report. Over time, they just accepted being chewed out as part of the program. All of the customer service improvements we were trying to make stopped once the stores reached this level. I had written the president a three-page letter detailing what I believed were the problems with the stores. I offered to have a meeting with him, which we did.

At this meeting, I told him that I worked seven days a week, not to impress him but to show him that we were very dedicated to helping our clients improve. He told me that he worked seven days a week and was not impressed. I felt my enthusiasm dissipate and I could see what the managers were up against. I wanted to point out that I was very involved in the business and that I knew what was going on in my clients' stores. When he said he wasn't impressed, I bit my tongue. I wanted to curse and say, "I'm not impressed with how you run this company." I finished with the meeting and we parted on good terms. My whole attitude about business changed after this meeting. I had worked really hard for this client, and it seemed like he couldn't care less. I then realized that no one else in business really cares about you, how hard you work, or what problems you have. I started to ask myself, "Why should I care more than my clients do about their own companies?" The answer is, I shouldn't. I did the job I was asked to do, to the best of my ability. That's all they can ask of me and that's all I can ask of myself.

After that day, I would ask myself, "Did I do my best?" If the answer was, "Yes" that's all I could do. Clients didn't pay us enough for me to worry about them at a barbecue or while reading the Sunday paper.

Unfortunately, your customers and clients do not take *your* company or feelings into account when making their business decisions. When I was in the process of selling my business, there was a two-store grocery outfit that we worked for. At one point I thought about not selling the business, but just paring down my accounts to a more profitable and manageable level. I struggled with how I could keep mystery shopping their two stores if I went with the latter decision. Their owner had dropped their old mystery shopping company in favor of us and I felt personally obligated not to let them down. There was also a shopper who had a rather difficult home life who shopped those two stores. I didn't want her to lose that income. I even overpaid her to do the stores just to "help out."

In the end, my concerns were for nothing. The owner of the two stores shocked me when she told me she sold her stores to her brother-in-law. The shopper, even though she did not have another job, thought the stores were too much trouble and didn't want to shop them anymore. A large part of the reason I wanted to keep the stores was because she had two kids and needed the money.

I'm not saying you shouldn't think about others and the consequences your decisions have on them, but it is doubtful that you come up in others' decision making.

POINTS TO PONDER

- Care about and do your job to the best of your ability, but not at the sacrifice of your family, friends, health, or your own happiness.

- If you're thinking about business when your head hits the pillow you're giving too much of yourself. I know, I've been there.

7

It's Lonely at the Top: Leadership for the First Time

"There are no bad soldiers, only bad officers."—**Napoleon**

"A business is a reflection of the leader. A fish doesn't stink just from the tail, and a company doesn't succeed or fail from the bottom." —**Gary Feldmar**

Leadership is a very difficult aspect of starting a business for new entrepreneurs. Aside from all the details of just getting the business going, as the owner and president of your company, you're going to spend time "finding your leadership self." This was difficult for me. I had been in charge of the "night crew" (graveyard shift) at A&P for several years, but I wasn't the store manager. When my eight hours were up, I went home. If I made a bad decision on my shift, "Well, I'm sorry" would pretty much cover it and it would either wait until the next night or someone else would have to pick up the slack. I was just an employee, and A&P was not going to rise or fall depending on what I did. In the end, I answered to the manager who answered to his district manager who answered to his supervisors and so on. But, when you are in charge of your own company, there is no one to pick up the slack. You're on your own, and that's the scary part. You can't point to someone else and say, "That was Bob's idea." You are the ultimate decision-maker and the buck stops with you. There is a saying in the Yukon, "The speed of the leader determines the speed of the pack."

Responsibility is not the same as leadership. You may be twenty, brilliant, and the owner gives you the keys to the store when he is on vacation. That's not leadership. It's a start, but again, the ultimate responsibility is not yours. You still have a boss you answer to. Leadership is an animal all it's own. It's a little scary when you become "The One." You have to *want to lead.* If you're talented but afraid to be in charge or make decisions, you should work for someone else. Even with a small business, I had trouble finding my way through the leadership maze. We had, at that time, three employees and about fifty independent contractors working for us, and I wasn't always sure how I wanted to act. Was I going to be stern, no nonsense, and aloof? Was I going to be extremely approachable and a big brother to all? Was I going to be laid back? Was I going to be very hands-on? Was I going to be a rah-rah type? Was I going to portray a young and brash leader or a wiser, methodical one?

Another problem entrepreneurs have is that you can't be everyone's friend. If you have ten employees, there's that temptation to be popular rather than in charge. At some point, you will have to lay down the rules since you're in charge. It would be great if all your employees loved you, but that shouldn't be your main objective. You want your employees to do their jobs well. If you treat everyone like they're a best friend, when you have to take charge, they're going to wonder, "What got into him all of the sudden? Big boss man." If you get too buddy-buddy with your employees without them realizing they are accountable to you, they will walk all over you, and it will be very difficult for you to get back control. Leadership is not a popularity contest. Employees don't necessarily have to like you, but they need to respect you. That is a key distinction that new entrepreneurs have to remember.

I have identified several traits that *all* good leaders share, regardless of their personal style.

- **Good communication skills.** An effective leader has to be able to get everyone in the organization on the same page. Employees have to know what they are supposed to do and why they are doing it. The best example of a problem I had with this was communicating my business ideas to my wife when we were working together. She made many mistakes and would say, "I thought you would want this first instead of that." It was frustrating, but *it was my job to get her to understand,* and not her job to figure me out. Winston Churchill is a good example of a leader that communicates effectively. Would you have any doubts where he stood after this quote, "Never give in. Never, never, never, never! Never yield in any way great or small, except to convictions of honor and good sense?" With a statement like that, there was no ambiguity. The people knew where he stood and what the goal was. An important thing to remember is that you don't have to be a Churchill or Knute Rockne to fire up your troops and be a good communicator. Instead, believe in your company's goals and visions and speak it, write it, repeat it, live it. Former CEO of Johnson and Johnson, Jim Burke, estimated that he spent forty percent of his time communicating the J&J credo.

- **Focus.** When a company sets its sights on too many targets, they won't hit any of them. This is a problem I see with many new entrepreneurs. I have spoken with many new business owners and often they have lots of great ideas. Their problem is that they try to implement all those great ideas at once. On Monday they'll start with one idea. On Tuesday, they'll work on the second idea because it's such a great idea and it can't wait, even though they haven't followed through on the first idea. Their days aren't as effective because they were split in too many directions. Winston Churchill lends another great example. In 1940, speaking of Britain's mission, he said, "Our whole people and empire have vowed themselves to the single task of cleansing Europe of the Nazi pestilence and saving the world from the new dark ages. We seek to beat the life and soul out of Hitler and Hitlerism. That alone. That all the time. That to the end." This is a great example of a clearly stated goal that was effectively reached. Why did the United States lose the war in Vietnam? Because there was no clearly stated goal or focus. How could we win when people asked, "Why are we here?"

- **Decisiveness.** This is something I think I do well. A leader has to be able to make decisions and stick with them. That doesn't mean that if you make a mistake you have to ride it all the way to the end. You have to be flexible and adjust your course along the way. What you can't do is say you're going with strategy *A* on Monday and on Friday put that strategy on hold. Two weeks later you say you are going with a modified version of *A*, but later that week you again say you're putting the brakes on *A* until so and so happens. The employees won't know what they're doing, whether they are coming or going. Sometimes a hard decision has to be made and you won't know until the end if it was a good or bad one. It doesn't matter. Move on. Dwight D. Eisenhower nearly blew D-Day because he could not make up his mind on the best moment for the attack. Finally, he said, "No matter what the weather looks like, we have to go ahead. Waiting any longer could be even more dangerous. So let's move on." Everyone has made bad decisions. What most people don't realize is that not deciding is a decision. You've decided to do nothing and that's how companies and organizations stagnate. Another mistake people make is "paralysis by analysis." Sometimes people will go over information for so long, the pros and cons, the ins and outs, that they never make a decision. In today's over-informed society, there is always another piece of information out there to analyze. No one can possibly analyze every piece of information.

- **Accountability.** It's lonely at the top. There is no one else to make the decisions for you. When you make a bad decision, *you have to take the blame.* You can't blame your mistake on the marketing and accounting departments. It was your mistake. Everyone makes mistakes and your employees will accept the fact that you make them, too. But people will not follow you or believe in you if only take credit for the good decisions. Maybe a middle manager can get away with placing blame on someone else, but a CEO will lose all credibility. Remember that a good leader should take less of the credit and more of the blame than he deserves.

- **Honesty.** Having been both a leader and an employee, I know what it's like to be in both positions. There is nothing that will make the followers lose faith in their leader quicker than dishonesty. A leader may lie to his employees for many different reasons. Even if the goal is a positive one, it is unacceptable to lie to your employees. I don't believe that the "end justifies the means." Employees will very quickly lose respect for a leader or manager that they feel is lying to them. Then it will be very hard to restore their faith in you.

- **A Belief in the Objective.** To me, this trait more than any other, is the most important quality of an effective leader. We've all heard the phrase, "lead by example." Believe it or not, this simple solution can be one of the most effective ways of leading employees. A true belief in a common goal will permeate the company from the top down.

- **The Ability to Delegate.** When you first start out, you might be tempted to do everything yourself, to be involved in every decision. Effective leaders pick out good "generals" and let them do their jobs. It is important to be informed, but you can smother employees if you're constantly looking over their shoulders. If you don't feel that someone can do the job on their own, without constant supervision, they shouldn't be working for you.

In the end, you have to be what your personality lets you be. If you're quiet and shy, you're not going to be a good rah-rah type and you shouldn't try to be. It is an evolving process. You don't wake up one morning and just become a General Patton or Prime Minister Margaret Thatcher (the "Iron Lady") type. It will take time to find yourself. Remember that your leadership style sets the tone for the whole company.

POINT TO PONDER

- There is not one correct leadership style. Ghandi and General Patton had completely opposite styles, but both were effective leaders because they were good communicators, were focused, decisive, honest with those under them, and they strongly believed in their objectives. Find the style that's right for you and stick with it.

8

Learn the Art
of Self-Promotion

"If I am not for myself, who, then, will be for me?"—**Hillel, philosopher**

I am naturally shy and on the quiet side. I don't like to talk about myself but if I do, I prefer to keep it modest. I would rather let my actions do the talking. That's how I was in the beginning of my business. When I had only a client or two, I didn't even tell people I owned a business. I figured the company was too small to even bother mentioning. I slowly realized, though, that if I didn't promote my company, no one else would.

Every day you read about companies in the newspaper and most of the time it's a result of PR. A big company like General Motors is always in the news, sometimes by their choice, sometimes not. The small companies, though, have to actively seek out publicity. I quickly realized that reporters don't find you, you have to go to them, often several times before they are interested. Reporters like to write about companies or people that have already been written about. Several times I had publications call me based on articles they read elsewhere. Reporters figure, if publication *A* wrote about you, you must be newsworthy. This has a tendency to snowball. You were written about in publications *A, B,* and *C,* so now *D* is interested too. After *D, E* asks if they can interview you, too. It feeds off itself.

Two companies can be completely the same, but reporters are going to interview the one that is actively promoting itself. I learned this first hand. I was sending out press releases one December to connect mystery shopping with the fact that everyone would be holiday shopping. I sent out about fifty press releases to various New Jersey papers. I also took a chance and sent one to *The New York Times*. I figured the only thing I had to lose was a stamp. In the beginning of January, a *Times* reporter called my office (still in our house). She said she received our press release and would like to do an article on mystery shopping. She asked if she could go out with one of our shoppers. She did and we were the featured company in the mystery shopping article. My heart did back flips when I saw the positioning of the article: front-page center of the business section with a picture of one of our shoppers. It was quite a rush. Later that morning, *PrimeTime Live* called and was interested in doing a story. That's the magic of PR. It was all because of a press release that I wrote and a thirty-three-cent stamp. Unfortunately, we did not make it onto *PrimeTime Live*, but hey, they're not calling anyone else I know either.

There were about five hundred mystery shopping companies in the industry when that article was written. We were the featured company because we contacted the reporter and made ourselves available. There were companies a hundred times the size of mine, but the reporter had never heard of them. To her, C&S was as big as she needed for the article. It gave us instant credibility. To most people, if the *Times* thinks you're important enough to write about, who are they to think otherwise? I brought a copy of that article to all future meetings with prospective clients. That usually erased any doubts they had about us or mystery shopping in general.

Anyone who can spell and has a computer and printer can do PR. *It is that easy.* My only background in PR, before I started my company, was taking two classes at Rutgers. I met with a fancy PR agency in Princeton, NJ, after I had already gotten our company featured in the *Times* and *Vogue*. They were impressed with my results, but gave me all the reasons why I needed to do it professionally. Some of their reasons had merit, but not enough to justify a $5,000 a month retainer. It's OK to look into what a PR firm can do for you, but don't let them intimidate you into thinking you can't do it yourself. If they didn't make it seem like only a well-trained professional with many contacts could do public relations, they couldn't justify charging you $150 per hour. Also, don't worry if your company is small. When I got coverage in my first two articles, I had no revenue at all. When your company reaches the size of Intel, then you hire outside professionals. Until then, I will give you eleven tips, that if followed correctly, I guarantee will get you press.

1. *Don't be intimidated about dealing with the media.* Most people have an interesting story if they put the right slant on it. An important thing to remember is that media outlets *need stories* and *they appreciate getting press releases on good stories.* Ever wonder how Mr. Jones got his pharmacy written about over all the other pharmacies out there? He let a reporter know that he was available and he told the reporter about his story in a press release.

2. *Public relations does not have to be expensive.* I sent my first press release to *The New York Times* on a single white sheet of paper in a hand written envelope. What mattered was *what I wrote* on that paper. If you are ever asked to send a press kit, it will cost you about five dollars. Include in it any pertinent articles you've appeared in, including a biography of yourself and a fact sheet about your company. On the fact sheet, include what it is that your company does and what makes it different from its competitors. You can also include sales figures, the size of your company, and any important achievements by you or your company. A kit can also include an 8×10 photo of yourself.

3. *Go to the library and borrow a book on PR.* Learn the proper format for a press release. Most people get too fancy because they are trying to stand out. Instead they stand out as amateurs. A white piece of paper, in the proper format, with something interesting written on it, will get a response. Reporters do not have much time, and they don't appreciate gimmicks.

4. *Unless you've discovered the cure for cancer, start small.* You will want to contact your college paper, the local newspaper, and the free one you find in your mailbox. These are easy to get into and will give you practice dealing with reporters. After these, go to the next level of publication, the regional newspaper or magazine. After that, you can keep going bigger. The idea is to build a portfolio of articles. You will be able to show these articles to prospective clients and other reporters and say, "See how many people have written about us."

5. *When you do get called by a reporter, bend over backwards to accommodate them.* Usually the easier you make their life, the better the article will come out. Also, I was always trying to figure out what the reporter's slant would be. Most of the time it was a straightforward, informational piece

about mystery shopping. Don't do any article or TV appearance that will put you in a bad light. I did not pursue the *PrimeTime Live* possibility, because I did not like the slant they wanted to take. Maybe there is no such thing as bad publicity for entertainers, but it can be devastating to businesspeople or their company.

6. *In four paragraphs, be able to write what makes you interesting.* What would make *you* pick up a paper and read about you? Also, make sure to customize your release to the publication you are writing to. *Modern Maturity* is not interested in your release about Generation X'ers starting their own companies. I have used every angle I could think of to fit into publications: The new entrepreneur, the interesting little company, the local kid who made it. If it doesn't fit into what their readers want to read, you won't get written about.

7. *Keep the adjectives to yourself.* Writing that your company is "truly amazing" or "revolutionary" will turn off a reporter. The reporter just wants to know what makes your story newsworthy. If they write about you, they can add their own adjectives.

8. *Don't badger publications or their reporters.* It is okay to be aggressive, but I've heard reporters complain that some companies send out so many press releases about non-issues that the reporters don't even take them seriously anymore. Often, you will have to wait for the right time to send your releases. Most publications, if asked, will give you an idea of future stories they're working on. You might have a great story about being a 20-year-old business owner, but if the magazine isn't doing their piece on young business people for three months, they're just not going to write about you now.

9. *Never say anything to a reporter that you don't want to see in print.* I once took a reporter from a New Jersey newspaper to a client's restaurant to give her a better feel for what we did. Unfortunately, the service was not very good and I commented on it. The reporter put my comments in her article along with the name of the restaurant. The owner of this New Jersey restaurant lived in Nebraska and he was not pleased when the article was eventually passed along to him. I was able to smooth over the situation with him, but I learned to watch what I say. You can talk with a reporter for

two hours and an innocent little comment could be the slant of their entire article.

10. *Good PR is worth a thousand times the costs of good advertising.* First of all, PR is virtually free. Second, a written article or TV appearance will give you *implied credibility.* Which do you find more impressive, a segment on *Dateline* or a commercial during it? PR also lasts forever whether it is in the newspaper, the radio, or on TV. For example, anyone who has ever been on *Oprah* or *The Tonight Show* will also put that in their byline, even if it was a fifteen-minute segment that aired five years ago. An ad just lasts as long as you pay to have it run.

11. *Be a quote source.* Maybe you can't think of an interesting slant or you really feel that you haven't done anything new or exciting that would be worth publicizing. You can still use your expertise in your field to help a reporter write a story. For example, maybe you are one of five hundred real estate agents in your city, and a reporter is doing an article on housing trends. The reporter would need to contact someone they can quote and get information from someone that is an expert on local housing trends. This is when you read in the paper, "Jane Smith, a realtor with ABC Realty, said, '. . .'" You would need to first contact that reporter or paper, and let them know that you wouldn't mind being called to help out with an article in your area of expertise. It's great publicity, and you can be used over and over again as a quote source.

I'll give you one bonus tip in dealing with the media. If a reporter writes about you, send them a thank-you note. You would be surprised how few people do this and how many reporters remember it. It doesn't matter the size of the publication either. *Always* send a thank-you note. The college student working for the school paper could be the future editor of *Newsweek.*

Two great examples of self-promotion are Howard Stern and Donald Trump. Think about how many DJs you can name outside of your area. Why is he the "king of all media?" Because he has called himself that enough times that others just started to repeat it. Now he's got a book, movie, number one radio show, a TV show, and he's unstoppable. How many real estate moguls can you name other than Donald Trump? None? Me neither. Donald Trump will hold a press conference for anything. He has reached the point where he is famous for just being Donald Trump. Most of the stories about him are now about his personal life. You've seen him in a Pizza Hut commercial and he had a cameo in the Little Rascals movie. Oh, he's also been a guest on the Howard Stern radio show.

PR is no replacement for being good. Many people say both Stern and Trump are very good at what they do, but then so are a lot of other people. The difference? They publicize it!

ACTION PLAN

- Everyone has an interesting story if you put the right slant on it. What is your slant? A 22-year-old pet shop owner could use several different slants: A new store in the area; how you share part of your profits with the local animal shelter; when most people are getting their first real jobs, you're starting a business; how your love of animals made this your dream.
- Think small instead of big when starting PR. Your first press will probably not be in *Fortune.* Start a database of newspapers and magazines in your area that might be interested in your story.
- When your school or local paper does interview you, ask the reporter for some advice. What caught their eye with your release? Can they think of any other angles for different types of media such as TV or radio? They won't mind answering a few questions as long as it doesn't turn into a PR 101 class.
- Don't be afraid to ask for referrals. Maybe the reporter knows someone at *XYZ* magazine that would love to report your story.

March 5, 1999

Contact: Mark Csordos, President
C&S Mystery Shoppers, Inc.
(555) 555-1212 (office)
(555) 555-1213 (fax)

FOR IMMEDIATE RELEASE

NEW JERSEY COMPANY GETS PAID TO SHOP

EAST BRUNSWICK: The employees of this company get paid to shop and eat all over the tri-state area, while the rest of us are scurrying around. That's what C&S Mystery Shoppers, Inc., based in East Brunswick, NJ, does. The biggest mystery to most people though is, "What is a mystery shopper?"

What a mystery shopper does is actually very simple. They pose as shoppers and rate their experience in a restaurant or retail store. The shoppers then fill out evaluation forms to detail what happened during their visit. The owners then use the data to increase the level of service they already provide their customers and ultimately increase their profits.

The idea for the company came when Mark and his brother received some bad service from a well known merchant. They realized that they received poor service quite often, but the owners never knew about it. Most people never complain, they just never return to that business. They researched it and found that, "96% of dissatisfied customers never complain, they just never go back to that place of business." They also realized that mystery shopping was a way to offer owners an objective look at how their employees treat their customers.

"It is hard to beat as a part time job," said Ann Sower, one of C&S Mystery Shoppers' 100 shoppers. "I can go to lunch at a restaurant then pick up some groceries at the supermarket and get paid to do it. It's fun work; you just have to make sure you're fair and accurate."

C&S's personal approach to mystery shopping has gathered this regional company national attention. Since February they have been featured in *The New York Times, Business Start-Ups* and *Vogue.* Mark Csordos was also picked for *New Jersey Monthly's* and *Business News New Jersey's* "40 Under 40" articles in the past year. Mark is a 1995 Rutgers graduate with a degree in Communications. Mark is also a contributing editor to the just released book on customer service, *Celebrate Customer Service.* C&S plans to offer more services in 1999, but for now, watch out. They just might be sitting next to you at a restaurant.

###

SAMPLE PRESS RELEASE

SECTION **2**

TIME AND EXPERIENCE

Time waits for no one. It is the most valuable commodity that anyone has. You and Donald Trump both have the same twenty-four hours a day to get things accomplished. It's what you do with those twenty-four hours that are important. No matter how much money Mr. Trump makes in his life, he will not get a second more than you get. Use your time wisely.

Experience is a hard teacher, but it could be the best one you ever have. One of the biggest mistakes people make is to not learn from the mistakes they've already made or from the mistakes of others. There is only one thing worse than making mistakes and that's not learning from those mistakes.

9

The Power of Goal Setting

"Our plans miscarry because they have no aim. When a man does not know what harbor he is making for, no wind is the right wind."
—**Seneca (4 BC–65 AD)**

If you don't have goals, you'll never accomplish anything. Period. It's as simple as that. If you think about it, how could you? If you don't have goals, you're not working towards anything. If you're not working towards anything, then why would your life ever be any better than it is at this very minute?

What most people have are wishes, not goals. I use the following example to illustrate the difference. If you and I went to the mall and asked the people we met what some of their goals are, a common one would be to retire financially independent by a certain age. We would then ask the following questions:

- How much money would you need to retire and by what age? What is your game plan for acquiring this money?
- Where will you invest—stocks, bonds, real estate, a combination?
- If retirement is twenty years away, what will you do about some of the obstacles you might face, such as paying for your kids' college tuition?
- What if the country goes into a recession?
- Who in your peer group will talk you out of that new luxury car and into something more inexpensive so that you can reach your financial goals?
- Why did you set this goal in the first place?
- What is your motivation for accomplishing it?
- How do you see the end result of this goal?

If we asked people these questions, we'd get mostly blank stares. The majority would admit that they never thought in that much detail. In reality, what these people have is a wish. They wish that someday, somehow, they'll be financially independent.

Maybe they work for the right company and have a good pension. Maybe their aunt will win the lottery drawing. But the truth is, they really have no idea how they'd do it. You know what? They won't.

First and foremost, ask yourself, "What is my goal? What do I want to do?" The next question is, "Is that realistic?" For example, if you're starting a new business and you want to do $100 million in sales in five years, that's probably unrealistic unless you are in a super growth industry and you have plenty of venture capital. One of the biggest mistakes people make with goal setting is setting unattainable goals. A goal should make you stretch farther than you've ever gone before but it shouldn't be so much of a stretch that no matter how hard you work, you won't be able to accomplish it.

Next, set a completion time for your goal. What you want to do is break your bigger goal down into smaller, more achievable goals. Writing a book can be a daunting task. You have some ideas, but you have to fill 196 pages in a logical order that a reader will find interesting. When writing my book, I broke it into smaller achievable tasks. I first did an outline with what I wanted to include. Then I started writing some of the chapters. Once the book was complete, it had to be proofread. I went back and revised the chapters and so on. Each task was small and doable. Just write an outline. Okay, I can do that. Start by writing some of the easier chapters. Okay, no problem there. I kept on this way until I had a finished book.

Next, what's your plan to accomplish your goal? You've set a realistic goal to reach two million in sales in the next five years. Now, how are you going to do that? Believe it or not, many people forget this section. They get all excited about having set a goal and want to rush out there and start working on it without giving any thought to exactly how they're going to get it done.

All this should be going down on paper. You wouldn't drive from New York City to San Francisco without first getting directions. You may make hotel reservations, and you would come up with a budget for gas, food, site seeing, etc. That is your goal plan—your map for getting from where you're starting to where you want to go.

The last part is to visualize the end result. To be successful you need to believe that you can truly accomplish your goal. With the mystery shopping, I pictured us going into stores and restaurants all over New Jersey. With the book, I pictured it on

Amazon.com and signing books at a bookstore. I pictured the end result and worked every day to make that vision a reality.

A lack of goal setting is the biggest problem I find with the people I meet. They have no direction in life, and if they have a direction, they have no map to get them there. Everyone wants to be financially independent, but few ever make it. Lots of people want to start a business, but all they do it talk about it in general ways. They use generalities like "someday" and "maybe if." If you want to live a better life, whatever you envision that to be, you have to set goals and develop a plan to achieve them.

POINTS TO PONDER

- You can't work on more than a few goals at a time. This is one of the biggest mistakes I see people make. They don't have priorities. You may make a list of a hundred things you want to accomplish, but you can't work on them all at once. You need to pick the one, two, or three most important goals you have and work on them. You may not ever have the time to work on all of your goals, so it's important to start with the ones that have the highest priority in your life.

- Find a peer group that will help you with your goals. You will probably set both big and small goals—"Clean out the garage on Saturday" and "Start a new business." With the bigger goals, have people around that know what you are trying to accomplish and will help and support you.

10

Knock, Knock–
It's Opportunity

"Most of the things worth doing in the world had been declared impossible before they were done." —**Louis D. Brandeis**

"The dawn does not come twice to awaken a man." —**Arabic proverb**

"Nothing is more critical to a businessman than the ability to recognize and exploit opportunities." —**Jean Paul Lyet, former CEO of Sperry Corporation**

Everyday on the street, standing in line next to you, or making small talk at the water cooler are those people who feel they have no choices in life. They feel trapped. Their current position is where they'll stay forever. I believe we all have an infinite amount of options if we just look around us. One never knows when opportunity will knock, but by most accounts, it only knocks once. If you don't answer the door, without question, someone else will. And for you, that will lead to the age-old question of—"What could have been?"—four truly sad words.

A life-changing opportunity usually involves risk, which is why most people hesitate when the chance arises. Risk is a part of being an entrepreneur, but it is everywhere else, too. It is unavoidable. You could die in a car accident or hit your head slipping in the shower. Don't be afraid of risk. It keeps things interesting and helps keep you sharp and focused. Risk is not what some people think, such as jumping out of an airplane without a parachute. That's plain stupid. You have to weigh your options and see what can be gained and/or lost by seizing the opportunity.

Everyone's life comes to a crossroads at some point. Many times people will not take the opportunity because they feel it is not the right time. They just moved, they'll wait until they've saved more money, they want to start a family first, etc. I was twenty-four when I graduated from Rutgers University. My opportunity was starting a mystery shopping company. I was going to get married in a couple of months and I had a secure job. My father told me not to quit my job with a new wife and a mortgage. Some suggested I work part time on the business until I had more clients, but I knew I wouldn't get more clients unless I had the time to pursue them. If I had waited, I would probably still be waiting. Waiting until we move into our new home. Waiting until after our first child is born. Waiting until I save enough money. That's what most people do. They wait without realizing the opportunity is long gone. Opportunity has moved on to others who are ready to accept it. One day most people wake up and realize *that **was** the best time.* Now they have two kids going through college and twenty-three years with the same company. How can they quit to chase a dream now?

I'm going to share with you a non-business story of someone we have all heard of and let you imagine how his life would have been different if he did not take the chance at his one opportunity.

A studio wanted to buy his script for a sports/love story, but didn't want this unknown actor to star in it. They already had many famous actors in their stable. At one point, the studio offered this unknown the equivalent of $2 million in today's money for the script, as long as someone else was the star. Our hero said of the offer, "So I did a lot more soul-searching. Intellectually, you're a fool if you don't take the money. But emotionally, I said, 'Could I live with myself for the rest of my life knowing I sold off the script and didn't stay with the project?' I was 29. It was the time; it was now or never because I knew that this opportunity would never come again." The studio finally relented, with contingencies, to let Sylvester Stallone star in *Rocky. Rocky* went on to win the Oscar for best picture and Stallone became a household name.

I think opportunity must be coupled with perseverance. Many famous people would not have had opportunity knock if they hadn't persevered long before it came calling. They kept plugging away until the road of perseverance met with opportunity. An entire book could be written about those who did not give up. (The following are from *Speaker's Library of Business,* Joe Griffith, p. 250)

- Henry Ford failed and went broke five times before he finally succeeded.
- Eighteen publishers turned down Richard Bach's 10,000-word story about a "soaring" seagull, *Jonathan Livingston Seagull*, before Macmillan finally published it in 1970. By 1975, it had sold more than 7 million copies in the United States alone.
- Richard Hooker worked for seven years on his humorous war novel, *M*A*S*H*, only to have it rejected by 21 publishers before Morrow decided to publish it. It became a runaway best seller, spawning a blockbuster movie, and a highly successful TV series.
- Winston Churchill did not become Prime Minister of England until he was 62, and then only after a lifetime of defeats and setbacks. His greatest contributions came after he was a senior citizen.

I could go on and on, but you get the point. The list of people that gave up before their time is a million times longer and no one has ever heard of those people. I think perseverance is one of the hardest things about starting a new business: sticking around long enough for the fruits of your labor to pay off. How many lives would be different today if Henry Ford got a job after the first time he went broke? My wife and I would be driving different cars, at least. How would Richard Hooker's life be today if he stopped writing after five years or stopped looking for a publisher after ten rejections? Think about it. You work on something for seven years and twenty people reject it. In my own life, I went six months between getting my first and second clients. At one point, I was delivering newspapers so I didn't have to eat away at my savings. Only now, several years after I started my initial business, is all the work starting to finally pay off.

Recognizing and seizing opportunity are important but you have to be in the game to get the chance in the first place. You may be thinking about starting you're own business, just be ready to open the door when **your** opportunity comes knocking.

POINT TO PONDER

The following is one of the best examples of perseverance meeting opportunity and it always gives me the push to keep moving forward.

Age 22, failed in business
Age 23, ran for legislature and was defeated
Age 24, failed again in business
Age 25, elected to legislature
Age 26, sweetheart died
Age 27, had a nervous breakdown
Age 29, defeated for speaker
Age 31, defeated for elector
Age 34, defeated for Congress
Age 37, elected to Congress
Age 39, defeated for Congress
Age 46, defeated for Senate
Age 47, defeated for vice president
Age 49, defeated for Senate
Age 51, elected President of the United States
Abraham Lincoln

"Success seems to be largely a matter of hanging on after others have let go." —William Feather

---

11

Fail to Plan and You Plan to Fail (my third biggest mistake)

"For everything you must have a plan." —**Napoleon**

"If you don't know where you're going, you could wind up someplace else." —**Yogi Berra**

Several business advisors told me that the first thing I should do is write a business plan. Did I? Well, Sort of. With the help of a friend I did write several pages of what I was proposing to do with my mystery shopping company. There were two problems with the plan I wrote. First, I wrote it quickly just so I could say, "I have a plan." At best it was an outline, a rough sketch. It was better than nothing at all, but it lacked any real depth to guide me through the future. Second, I never read it. I just kept it in a drawer. It's like writing directions from New Jersey to California and leaving them in the glove compartment during the drive. I wrote some company goals in my plan and when I went back several months later to read the plan, we missed all of them. What did I expect? I never paid attention to them and didn't really have any idea how to get them accomplished.

Business plans are different things to different people, but all good business plans include the following:

- **Describe your business.** You're not the only one who will read your business plan. As your company grows, your executives will need to refer to it, and if you ever need a loan from investors or a bank they will want to know exactly what you do. For example, Dell sells computers, Ford manufactures cars, and Gap sells clothes.
- **Mission statement.** A mission statement should be a one-paragraph summary of a company's purpose, goals, and values. Your mission statement often defines your business.

- **Market analysis.** What is the size and projected growth rate of your industry? Your market should be broken down into segments that include the age, income, product type, geography, buying patterns, customer needs, and other classifications that relate to your industry.
- **Sales plan.** What makes your product special? You should be able to answer why a customer will pick your product over other brands. You will also need to answer how you plan to sell your product—retail, wholesale, Internet, mail order, discount, or phone orders. Will you need to maintain a sales force, and if so, how will they be trained and compensated?
- **Financial statements.** There are certain numbers, regardless of the business you're in, which are vital to track. They include break-even analysis, profit and loss, cash flow, and a balance sheet.
- **Executive summary.** A business plan should also define objectives and outline the course of action to achieve those objectives. The executive summary is the key to the rest of the plan. Get it right or your target readers will go no further. The best length is a single page. Emphasize the main points of your plan and keep it brief.
- **Exit plan.** Most people that start a business are so concerned about if the business will make it that they never stop to think about what happens when their vision comes true. After all, you start a business with the idea it will succeed, but what then? Are you going to take the company public? Will you leave it to your heirs? Will you sell it after five years? You need to answer, "What is all of this leading up to for me?"

In the beginning, your business plan doesn't need to be more than a couple of pages. I met with one business owner who spent $50,000 to have professional help writing and developing his plan. His company was well established, though, and did several million dollars a year in sales. When you're first starting out, if your plan answers the following few questions, you should be off to a good start: What are you selling? Why does the world need this product? How will you produce and sell it and to whom? How much do you have to sell it for to break even and to make a profit? In the beginning, as you grow and start to learn your business, you'll constantly be adding to and refining your plan. Don't think of your plan as too time consuming. It is meant to be a document that is used often. Using the example of driving from New Jersey to California, most travelers would continually check their map to make sure they're going in the right direction. Maybe when they reach Kansas, they find a shorter route and revise their plan.

Most of my business plan was in my head, which mean't no one, including myself, had access to it. I just had a vague notion, a general idea, of where I was taking the company. Problems had to be solved on the spot instead of having been prepared for. Key questions about the company I had not thought out included: What was I going to do to grow the company? How were we going to handle that growth? How and when was I going to replace my wife with a real office manager so that we could start a family? What would the company and I do if I got seriously hurt or sick?

I got lucky. I didn't really have a plan, but with hard work, my company prospered. But my lack of planning meant that we had to work harder to achieve the same results. If I had kept with my mental plans of doubling the business every year, we would have busted at the seams.

It doesn't matter if you'll be the only employee or if you plan to do five million dollars in sales your first year—learn from my mistake and write a business plan.

ACTION PLAN

- Buy business plan software. You can get a good program for under $100 that will take you through each step of the process.
- Once you've written your plan, ask some impartial people to read it and give their advice. They can give you an objective opinion. It is easy to write that you'll gross a million dollars the first year, but does your overall plan support that projection?
- Each time you make changes, give copies of your revised plan to all the key employees in your company. Continually revise your plan as new opportunities or unexpected situations arise.

12

Work on the Business, Not in It (my second biggest mistake)

"Don't do anything someone else can do for you." —**Bill Marriott Sr.**

"Ross Perot, CEO of the Perot Group, said, 'I surround myself with smart people, and I tell them what the goal is but I never give them any kind of checklist.' I say, 'Next year, we're going to the moon. You're in charge.' That's how John F. Kennedy approached the lunar launch. He said, 'Within ten years, we're going to put someone on the moon.' He never told anyone how to do it, but it happened anyway." —**Wess Roberts, Ph.D.,** *Leadership Secrets of Attila the Hun*

Not delegating was probably the second biggest mistake I made, behind hiring family members. *I spent too much time working in the business, not on the business.* Working in the business would be like owning a McDonald's and flipping the burgers yourself. Working on the business would be looking into getting a second franchise and developing your restaurant's business plan.

Unfortunately, that's what I did. I worked in the business. In the beginning, it might be impossible not to. You will probably be tight on money and you can't afford to hire people. If you're lucky enough to get five million in venture capital, you can get some employees, but most companies don't start like that. More companies start in someone's garage than with investor's money. So on day one you're the president, vice president, salesperson, janitor, gopher, etc. *My mistake was that I didn't drop some of these roles once I got the chance.* I'm not sure why, honestly. Part of the reason I did this was that I didn't want to spend what little money we had by hiring additional employees. I also had a hard time giving up control of things that I had done from the beginning. I later realized that type of short-term thinking was foolish.

I would do many of the mystery shops myself. As an example, let's say they take about forty-five minutes to do and ten to fifteen minutes to write up the report. If I did five shops on a Tuesday, including travel time, that was an eight-hour day. I was doing nothing to grow my business. I was doing work that I could have paid an independent contractor seventy-five dollars to do. I would also proofread other reports and sometimes personally fax them over to clients. This was something that a smart high school student could do. Meanwhile, I was the only person who would be able to sell our service to new clients. I didn't get much of a chance to do this because I was always working on the day to day stuff. There were a couple of times I was able to focus on growing the business and low and behold it worked! We would go through periodic growth spurts. But then I would make the same mistake again. I would work on servicing these new clients instead of getting shoppers to physically do the shops and free me up. When I was finally able to free myself to be a salesman again, I would repeat the growth process—get some new clients and then work on servicing them. It's a tough way to grow a business.

I finally did hire an employee after we got an outside office. My wife needed help getting reports out to clients by Monday morning; we were tired of working until midnight on Sundays to get the reports out. When we hired our employee, I didn't direct her correctly. Part of my problem was that my wife was not very good at her job, and she was not able to direct the employee correctly. One day, though, the absurdity of not delegating hit me. My wife and our part-time employee were working and I was sent to Wendy's to get lunch. Not as an ego thing, but I thought to myself, "Why am I the one getting lunch?" I had just been in *The New York Times* and I should have been using that PR in selling to new clients and growing the business. Instead I'm waiting in line to buy a pita combo. This was something that a sixteen-year-old with a car could do. I realized then that I was hopelessly *working in the business.*

I have given you my story and I will share with you a short story about one of the world's most famous business men who also learned the hard way to delegate.

Henry Ford once took over all the decision making at Ford Motor Company. He even set spies about to try to catch his managers actually making decisions on their own. Eventually his company crashed, and it was fifteen years before Ford showed a profit again.—Joe Griffith, *Speaker's Library of Business*

There are two ways you can avoid getting stuck working in the business. The first way is by hiring good people and learning to delegate. We had about a hundred independent contractors doing shops for us. We took the time to get the right type of shoppers, meet them, and teach them the process. Over the years we had very few problems with the shoppers. It made a big difference taking the time to get quality shoppers. If they said they would do a shop at 10:00 AM on Tuesday, we did not have to worry about them not showing up or doing it incorrectly. We had little turnover in shoppers and rarely had to do much training after the initial meeting. That is directly what Ross Perot is discussing in the opening quote. Hire good people and let them do their job. If you don't trust your underlings to do their job well, you need new employees.

I personally worked for a company that would hire any warm body, and they got what they paid for. When I worked the night shift for a grocery store they had no screening process. If you were breathing, you were hired. I worked with alcoholics that came to work drunk, drug users, and convicted felons. I wish I was exaggerating, but sometimes you did have to watch your back. A friend of mine had one man on his crew who couldn't read. He would literally compare the cans of cat food to find the matching ones when he was loading the shelf. What kind of quality did we have? Often, we had very little quality. One employee would be there one night and gone the next. A week later we'd find out that he had been arrested. And the company's performance? During the greatest bull market in the country's history their stock price was half of what it was ten years after I had started with the company. Hiring the right employees, whether a start-up or an established company is crucial to long-term success. Take the extra time and money to find the right employees, then let them do what you hired them to do. I've wondered how much extra money it cost that grocery store to have the revolving door policy with employees rather than to just pay a qualified person two or three more dollars an hour to do the job right.

The second part of not working in the business is to put systems in place where people can easily slide in and out of roles.

When my wife and I had two part timers in the office I wanted to put in a system that allowed us to know exactly where we stood with completed shops at any time during the week. It involved two spreadsheets. One was for scheduled shops during the week, which would include the shopper's name, and the day and time the shop was scheduled to be done. After a shop was completed, it was to be bolded, with the actual day and time typed in. If it wasn't in bold in the spreadsheet, it meant it hadn't been done yet. The second spreadsheet was called our pay sheet. It was supposed to be completed at the end of every day. It had much of the same information as the other spreadsheet and also included the store's score, if the report had been proofread, and whether or not it had been sent to the client. In theory, anyone should be able to look at the two spreadsheets and know exactly what stores had been shopped and which ones still needed to be shopped for the week. In practice, this didn't happen. As I have already stated, my wife was not good at running the office, and she often fell behind. If she were to take a day off, everybody else would have to do extra work to figure out what point we were at. This was the kind of thing that made me work in the business and not on it. Instead of looking at the spreadsheets for five minutes and then going to make sales calls, I would have to look on the computer to see what had been done or call my wife and ask her. It was all a waste of time and took my focus away from growing the business. I did the same thing with sales calls. I sometimes had a part-timer call businesses to find out if the company would be interested in mystery shopping and if so, the name of the contact person. What I would often get would be scraps of paper with names, notes, and addresses scribbled on them. It would sometimes take me as long to decipher the information as if I had just called the companies myself. Now, if someone makes calls for me, as soon as they get off the phone, they put that information in a database with any important notes. With systems in place, you'll do less managing of the little things, which will allow you more time to focus on the important things. It doesn't matter what type of business you run. They all need systems. Take a restaurant, for example. How do you efficiently get the order from the wait staff to the cooks and from the cooks to notify the wait staff when it's prepared? It takes a system. If you've ever waited forty minutes for your meal or received the wrong dish at a restaurant, it's a systems breakdown.

If your goal is to create a lasting company you need to have systems in place where people can be used interchangeably and new employees will fit in easily. If you create an environment where your company couldn't survive without you or other key employees, you will not be able to achieve any long-term success.

POINTS TO PONDER

- Don't be afraid to delegate and give orders. You may think you're saving money by doing much of the work yourself, but in the long run, it hurts the growth of the business.

- When hiring or promoting an employee, determine their strengths and weaknesses and how they would fit into your company or the new position. Although it may be tempting in the beginning, don't hire someone simply because they are available.

13

Everything Costs Twice as Much, Takes Twice as Long, and Yields Half the Results You Expect

"Time is the scarcest resource, and unless it is managed nothing else can be managed." —**Peter Drucker**

A friend of mine told me that everything costs twice as much, takes twice as long, and yields half the results you expect. Why this always seems to be true, I'm not quite sure. It's like the law of gravity. I'm not sure how it works, but I know if I jump out a window, I'm going straight down. I think the biggest advantage I get from remembering this little "business law" is to always temper my expectations and have a contingency plan ready.

I remember my first experience with this concept. We had just started to work with Manhattan Bagel, a fast-growing company based in South Jersey. We started working with a handful of corporate owned stores in New Jersey, but there were also several hundred franchised stores in the surrounding states. When I had spoken to the vice-president we had talked of possibly doing mystery shopping in *all* the stores, both company and franchised. Unfortunately, at this time, Manhattan Bagel was growing so fast that they had many ideas that never went anywhere. Regardless, I went back to my office (still the spare bedroom) with a calculator. I multiplied several hundred stores times the amount per shop times fifty-two weeks a year. It was simple. Within a few months, my salary alone would be six figures based just on Manhattan Bagel. In actuality, we billed Manhattan Bagel about ten thousand dollars that year. It was a far cry from the several hundred thousand I was hoping for. As it turned out, Manhattan Bagel later declared bankruptcy, and we actually received only a portion of what was owed to us.

I had a similar experience with a supermarket client. They were a co-op, which is similar to a franchise. There was one parent corporation and each store or group of stores were owned by different people. They wanted to do a test program with mystery shopping to try it out and see how the program went. I'll spare you all the details but the program started late, involved only half the number of stores that were originally discussed, and we billed only forty-five percent of what I originally projected. Again, a big difference in sales from what I had initially expected.

As a new entrepreneur, you may be inexperienced in estimating costs and projecting revenue, having had little business experience on which to base your figures. I also think that people tend to use either the best or worst case scenarios when estimating, when reality is usually somewhere in between.

Similarly, when it comes to costs, always have an emergency fund. No matter how accurately you budget or estimate you should always factor in at least 10% extra for unknown occurrences. I have found, also, that the larger the project, the later it will start, the longer it will take, and the more off-estimate it will become. I wanted an outside company to come in and network our office computers. Several companies quoted us a price over the phone for the work, but didn't mention all the extras we would have to purchase in addition to their quoted price. Unfortunately, there is nothing you can really do to avoid this. Just keep it in mind when budgeting resources. It seemed our clients always requested an additional meeting, another shop, a summary they never mentioned when setting up the program, etc.

The last part of this equation is time. Even when companies want and need your service, it's often a long period between the initial meeting and when the work begins. I was meeting with the president of a large company about my goal setting/time management workshop. He joked with me that he had relatives visiting and that he was working five half days but getting the same amount done. Then he realized, as he was saying this, why they needed a time-management workshop. In my mind I thought, "Sold!" It was still three months between that meeting and the time I was standing in front of his employees giving my workshop. This, despite the fact that he was the only decision-maker, and he wanted the workshop.

In our instant gratification culture, we are so used to things happening immediately, but unfortunately business doesn't work like that. Deliveries aren't always on time, meetings get cancelled, and people change their minds. Learning this lesson sooner, rather than later, will save you a lot of headaches in the future.

POINT TO PONDER

- In business, expect the unexpected—it usually happens.

14

The Best Advertising Really Is a Satisfied Customer

"I'll tell you the man who has the idea of service in his business will never need to worry about profits. The money is bound to come. This idea of service in business is the biggest guarantee of success that any man can have." —**Henry Ford**

"There is only one boss. The customer. And he can fire everybody in the company from the chairman on down, simply by spending his money somewhere else." —**Sam Walton**

I could write a whole book on customer service and someday I plan to. Coming from a business such as mystery shopping, where we evaluated customer service for a living, I know just how important it is. In this chapter I will cover several basic customer service concepts. They seem simple, but they are so often ignored. (If they weren't, I'd have to find a different line of work!) Why? Many times companies lose track of what made them successful in the first place—doing their job well. Sometimes they don't care. Other times they want to give good service but don't know how. Some companies don't know what makes good customer service. Whatever the reason, the smaller the company, the more important customer service. That means for anyone just starting out, great service is everything. Let's face it, no one wants to lose a customer. But if you have a problem with, say, Sears, and you cut up your credit card and vow never to go back, they'll never miss you. Granted, if enough customers do that, it will eventually affect a company even the size of Sears. You, on the other hand, can't afford to lose even one customer because of bad service. If you earn a bad reputation in the beginning, you might not last long enough to repair it.

I always see articles in the paper about how many businesses go belly up within the first five years and the reasons why (bad location, not enough capital, too much competition). I think customer service is an overlooked killer of businesses, *which leads to those other problems.* I had a bagel store within walking distance of my house. When I first moved into the neighborhood I ate there and received average food and unfriendly service. I'm sure other customers had the same problem because within a year they were out of business. In its place was a new bagel store with the same average food and bad service. They, too, were gone a year later. I'm sure if I asked the owners what happened, I'd get the usual—bad location, poor sales, etc. What you won't hear is, "We didn't treat our customers well enough." If customers tried their shop once and didn't return because of poor service, *that's why sales were disappointing, and that's what gives the appearance of a bad location.*

Here are what I consider to be the most important customer service keys to follow right from the beginning:

1. *Great customer service, and a strong belief in it, has to come from the top.* I have seen company presidents complain about their stores' customer service yet they themselves have no business courtesies at all. Some of these presidents can't be bothered to talk to customers when they are in the stores. They think, "That's someone else's job. I'm too important." What happens, though, is that others in the company see this and think, "If he's the president and doesn't want to be bothered with customers, why should I kill myself for $8 an hour?" This type of thinking will build a culture of indifference towards customers that will keep perpetuating itself as new employees are hired. I once had a store manager that would tell employees to tell customers that he was out, even though we all knew he wasn't. That store had terrible service because as employees we knew the manager didn't care, and he had a lot more invested in the company than we did.

2. *Do not treat customers differently depending on how much they spend.* Someone spending $5 today could be a $5,000 customer next month. My company used to work with a three-store supermarket chain. They actively used mystery shopping, but with only three stores they were one of our smaller clients. I gave them the same customer service and attention I gave our biggest client. One day I was rewarded. They recommended us to another company that was looking to do a two-day, statewide mystery shopping program. Those two days, though, were larger than

any *month's* revenue we'd ever had. Had we just been adequate, our client never would have recommended us. For a small company like ours, getting this project was like hitting the jackpot.

3. *Set yourself apart from your competition by the level of customer service you provide.* I would ask my supermarket clients, "If I'm having a barbecue Saturday and I want to buy my soda, paper plates, napkins, forks, spoons, hamburger buns, etc., why should I drive to your store? Every supermarket will have what I need and usually around the same price. What makes me go to your store and not the competitor?" If you ask yourself that question and you don't know the answer, you'd better figure it out pretty quickly. The answer usually is customer service. Sometimes a company's location or prices will blow everyone else away, but most of the time it comes down to service. Think about the places you shop and why you shop there. How often is the difference the service you receive? If you picked service more often than price or location, then you're like most people. Service counts.

4. *Don't nickel and dime your customers.* When I had a situation where we had an unhappy customer, I did what it took to right the situation. For example, if a client was unhappy with the quality of a report, I would either not charge them for it or do another one free of charge to replace it. I figured, "Why should I argue with a $10,000 a year client over something that costs me $50 retail?" What would I get? I'd get $50 and I'd have to worry about ticking off the customer and possibly losing a $10,000 a year client. When you think about customers, think about the *lifetime value* of that customer. For example, my wife and I are in our twenties. To a company like Sears, we could be a six figure customer over the years (TVs, VCR, washer and dryers, snow blowers, children's clothes, and on and on). Too often, though, companies only look at what you're buying that day. You have $33.81 in your shopping cart, so that's what you're worth to them. The way they should be thinking is $33.81 today, but the potential for another $99,966.19 in future sales. If you treat every customer like they're spending $99,000, your service will largely take care of itself. Unless a customer is trying to rip you off or is completely and utterly wrong, think about the dollars and not the nickels.

5. *Train your employees.* It sounds obvious, but I am always amazed when I encounter employees who can't even do the simplest part of their job. I went into a supermarket once and bought two ears of corn. The cashier rang them up as three. He was unable to void off the corn and ring it correctly. He let me walk away knowing he did not fix the problem because he did not know how. I used to be a cashier and one of the first things they taught us was how to do a void. How many times have you gone into a store, asked what you thought was a simple question, and no one could answer it? Companies avoiding training because it costs too much money. But, if you skimp in one place, it usually shows up somewhere else. The money the above-mentioned supermarket saved by skimping on training, they lost in future revenue because I will not go back there. No business has a shortage of competition that their customers can choose from.

6. *Don't lose sight of your customers as you grow.* This is a hard one. You're happy your company is growing, but in the beginning you will invariably spread yourself thin. You must not lose focus on what is propelling your growth in the first place—your customers.

7. *Service is more than just smiles.* I now live in the South where, overall, the service is friendlier than what I was used to in the Northeast. But being friendly is *only part of* providing superior customer service. Many companies think that if they're nice to customers then their service is good. But you also need to make sure mistakes don't happen and the customers' buying process runs smoothly. My very first night in North Carolina my wife and I went to a well-known restaurant chain. We ordered an appetizer and two main entrees. The restaurant got the appetizer and my dish incorrect. I say "the restaurant" because the waiter blamed it on the kitchen not reading the ticket correctly. The waiter was very nice and apologetic, but in the end my dinner was ruined because I only ordered two things and I didn't get either one. That restaurant needs a better system so that when the wait staff takes the order, the cooks process it correctly. The waiter told us that the cooks don't always read the tickets thoroughly, but that didn't solve my hunger. We have not gone back there since.

8. *Mind your manners.* It's a shame that companies have to even *think* about training new employees on common courtesy, but it's a sad reality. I'm talking about simple things such as, "Thank you," "Excuse me," and "You're welcome." It's such a small thing, but a lack of manners really stands out. I don't know how many times I have pointed out to store clerks that there was a spill in an aisle, there was an outdated product on the shelf, or a toilet was backed up, and got no response, not even a simple "thank you" for pointing it out. I'm just trying to make their job easier, but next time, even if I see aisle seven on fire, I'm not telling them. How many times have you spent quite a bit of money at a store only to have the cashier say nothing to you but the total? How appreciated do you feel by that company? One great thing about manners is that they *don't cost anything*. It doesn't cost a company a single penny when their employees use manners, but it sometimes costs them dearly when they don't.

9. *Monitor your customer service.* One fallacy that small business owners fall into is they feel that if they're on the premises they know everything that goes on. I always laugh inside when I hear this. Let's use a restaurant for our example and an owner that works twelve hours a day. How much time does she spend in the actual dining room observing her wait staff? After taking phone calls, attending meetings, scheduling, placing orders, and the fifty other things a business owner has to do, the answer is, "not much". What can she do to monitor her staff's service? Two things. One is to use mystery shopping. I'm not trying to be a shill for the industry, but it can be a wonderful tool to give an owner objective feedback about how the customers are being treated. And it is relatively inexpensive. Plus, you can mystery shop just about any type of business. Yes, even an Internet company! The second is to allow your customers a way to give you feedback, whether it be through your web site, with an 800 number, by posting your mailing address with contact person, through comment cards, or simply by asking them at the end how their experience was. Give customers the chance to communicate with you and make it easy to do so. Believe me, they'll let you know what they think of your service and product.

10. *Customer complaints are good.* I'm amazed at how many employees, including management, treat complaining customers like they have the plague. No one wants customers who are upset, but let's face it, companies are made up of people and people, even the best trained, do make mistakes. I'd rather have a customer complain to me and give me a chance to rectify the situation than tell all their friends and my competitor why they're not doing business with us anymore. Sometimes the complaints are frivolous and you just have to nod your head and say, "Yes ma'am, I understand." But sometimes the complaints will lead to product innovations. "Why don't you have this or do that?" And you're thinking, "Well, Ms. Customer, I never thought of that, but that's a good idea." Also, customers that complain are giving you a chance to keep them as customers. I complain often, although not as much as I could, and if a company gives a reasonable response to my complaint, I'll usually go back.

Customer service is not a cure-all, but it is what helps differentiate you from the competition. All the service in the world will not help you, though, if you overprice your products or have a poor plan in the beginning.

POINT TO PONDER

- Ninety-six percent of dissatisfied customers never complain about bad service; they just take their business elsewhere. Retaining only five percent more customers can make up to a seventy-five percent difference in your profits, not to mention the value of increased business due to referrals.

15

Charge What You're Worth (my fourth biggest mistake)

"A plumber was called to fix a leak. He looked at the pipe, gripped the hammer with both hands, struck the pipe as hard as he could, and the leak stopped. He presented the customer with a bill for $250.35. The owner was furious. 'This is outrageous: you were here only two minutes and all you did was hit the pipe.' The plumber itemized his bill: Wear and tear on the hammer–35 cents. Knowing where to hit–$250.00."
—Joe Griffith

One of the biggest mistakes I made was not charging clients what my service was really worth, thereby forcing my company to work harder than it had to. In the beginning, you'll probably have to price your service low to attract customers. When you start, price might be your only selling point since you don't have a track record. I practically *gave* Pizza Hut our service, but I had little choice. With them, I was looking for a client, but it was even better since they were a "name" client. I never actually figured it out, but we probably worked for Pizza Hut for break even or at a small loss. What we did get was experience, a reference, and the form that was the basis for all other point scoring forms we used in the future. I did the same thing with my second and third clients (Manhattan Bagel and a supermarket chain). I priced the service low and was happy to have the business.

My mistake came with the next clients I signed. Unlike the plumber in the example, I was afraid to upset clients and potential clients by charging them what our service was worth. I now had three happy name-brand clients (well-known in the tri-state area) and *I didn't raise my prices.* I also provided a service that made tangible improvements in their customer service and bottom lines. We were starting to get write-ups in local papers, and, with the name clients, we had credibility. Unfortunately, not until much later, and even then not to the full extent, did I raise our prices to match what the service was worth. The plumber knew that the homeowner could not fix his own pipes and charged him according to the years of training he had acquired to be able to fix a pipe in two minutes. I knew that my clients could not perform mystery shopping in-house nearly as effectively as I could, but I continued to charge them a bargain price.

I think I did this for several reasons. First, I did not do thorough market research. I had only a vague idea what other companies were charging for the same service. I went to a mystery shopping convention once and talked with a company owner who said I should have been charging twice as much for our shops. I was losing a large amount of potential revenue and profits just by not charging what my competitors were charging. I did raise our prices after that, but I did not come close to doubling them. Second, as a new entrepreneur, I was still wondering if I belonged. I had no previous business experience, and I wasn't sure if I was becoming a good businessman or just getting lucky. I had very little confidence. Unfortunately, my own insecurities as to whether my product was as good as "established" companies and if I really belonged as a business owner, kept me from charging what our service was worth. The third reason was that I was scared of giving my clients sticker shock. If they were used to paying X amount and I wanted to raise it fifty percent I'm sure that several clients would have dropped the service. And if they had? My attitude should have been, "So be it." With the extra money I would have been charging I could have made up the difference with future clients and the clients that took the price increase, and I would have been doing less work. Being young, though, I was afraid to upset anyone. I did not want them calling and asking me to justify the higher prices. They were happy and I was too eager to please. I should have realized I was not responsible for how others felt. We offered a good product and if they were upset at a price increase, they could go to a competitor that would charge them less.

There were other, less obvious, problems with undercharging our clients. We did not get the respect we deserved from the clients and sometimes the price was too low to be considered high quality (which it was). If I had been a lawyer that had two large write-ups in *The New York Times* and *Vogue,* I would have been charging my clients $350 an hour as an expert. Instead, clients often referred to me as "the mystery shopping guy." Unfortunately, customers (both service and retail) often equate the prestige of the product with the price tag.

If your price is too much lower than the competition or what the client perceives to be the value of the item, it often won't sell, no matter how good it is. This can happen to established companies as well as start-ups. A good example of under-pricing a product came from one of A&P's competitors. That supermarket had an all-purpose cleaner with exactly the same ingredients as the leading cleaner. It was priced so low, though, that it just languished on their shelves. They eventually had to pull their store brand even though it was identical to the leading brand, except in price, because customers *perceived* that the price was too low for the product to be of value.

I think there is a temptation, especially for young entrepreneurs, not to want to scare off potential clients. With few exceptions, your age and experience have no bearing on the price of your product or service. If you just started an advertising agency, you probably can't charge as much as an agency that has been around twenty years and has worked with Nike and Wal-Mart. But once you have a few satisfied clients that will give you references, you can raise your prices closer to those of your competitors. Don't be afraid to charge what you're worth. If you feel the product or service is worth $75, then charge the customer $75. Don't sell yourself short. There will always be a small percentage of people that simply want the lowest price available. Forget about them. Just deal with those that are willing to pay your fair price. Don't forget to figure in the value of your time. And remember, people and companies, *expect to pay for things.* I was once asked to speak at one of my client's meetings for a half-hour with about ten percent of their employees in attendance. I was going to charge them $250 for the talk until my wife suggested that we charge $400. They didn't blink an eye and the talk went very well. The client doesn't want to be gouged, but they do know that it costs to have an expert speak at their function. I was scared they would say, "$250 for you? No way!" But that was my own "headtrash" (see Chapter 27, "I Think, Therefore I Am") saying, "I'm not a professional speaker. What if I stink?" At $250, I also wasn't figuring in my travel time of two hours or preparation time for the speech. In the end, I was well worth the $400. The same goes for retail. A customer looking at a Lexus knows that they're going to pay $30,000–$40,000 for the car and they expect to. In this example, my client's need was to have me as a speaker at their event. The price was a secondary concern, if one at all.

Keep in mind that no one else worries if they charge you too much. Have you ever seen a doctor discount their bill or offer coupons? The phone company doesn't give you a break because you were talking to your sick mother. Some rock bands will charge $70 a ticket and feel *you should be happy to get one.* I knew one guy who charged his mother-in-law full price to landscape her lawn. He was just getting what his service was worth.

ACTION PLAN

- Identify what your competitor's charge for similar products and services. You do not want to set your prices too much higher or lower than what the market is paying.
- Identify what your break-even costs are and how much you will have to charge to make a profit.
- Identify who you want to target price-wise. A pen can cost anywhere from 20 cents to $20. For example, if you choose the high-end pen, you will need to price it according to what other high-end dealers are charging. If you sell your high-quality pen for 99 cents, it will be perceived as being of lower quality than the same exact, $20 pen because it is priced too much lower. Also, make sure to build some cushion in your price. Let's say my break-even point for a mystery shop was $20 per shop. I could price the shops at $22 per shop and make a profit but I had no room to maneuver. If a client wanted a better price, what could I lower it to? If we have to repeat a shop because of an error, it would take me ten additional shops to break even from this one. What if I had to pay my shoppers more, but I was locked into the $20 price?

16

Adversity Is a Great Teacher

"There is no education like adversity." —**Benjamin Disraeli**

"The very difficulty of a problem evokes abilities or talents which would otherwise, in happy times, never emerge or shine." —**Horace**

"We learn as much from sorrow as from joy, as much from illness as from health, from handicap as from advantage—indeed perhaps more." —**Pearl Buck**

No one really wants adversity. Life is obviously much easier on the days when everything falls into place. But I treat adversity like a special friend. It helps me grow and be a better person than I was the day before.

I have stated before how we struggled, both as a company and myself as a person, in the early days of the company. Luckily, I catch on quickly and we eventually went on quite a roll. We had been in *The New York Times* and it seemed every prospect I got in front of said, "Yes." Between the second and third year we more than doubled in sales. During this time, anytime I got in front of a prospect, I always felt they'd say, "Yes." The only problem with a situation such as this was that I wasn't learning anything. I wasn't growing as a businessperson, and I wasn't innovating my products at all. It was all becoming very easy.

I got my wake-up call from a supermarket chain in Pennsylvania. I got my opportunity to speak in front of them and had a great hour and a half meeting with three of their executives. They told me, and they were honest about it, that there was a second company that they were seriously considering. First, I thought they were bluffing. I thought they were trying to get me to lower my price. Second, I didn't think it mattered. I was thinking, "Hey, I was in the *Times*. I **know** supermarkets. My last ten prospects have said, 'Yes.' " Needless to say, I was overconfident. I was like a football team that beat up on weaker opponents. We might have had flaws in our game plan, but no one noticed because the team kept winning.

After a couple weeks of the supermarket "looking over the information," I got a call from one of their executives telling me they had decided to go with the other company. She was nice, but proceeded to tell me all the reasons they picked the other company over us. I was very surprised. It had been quite a while since we had been rejected. Obviously, it is not realistic to think that every lead or potential client will choose your company or product, and when one does say, "No," it affords you a great opportunity to learn. I didn't get this client, but she did spend the time to tell me what the other company had that we didn't. I could have taken this information in one of two ways, either by sulking or learning. I chose the latter. I could use what she told me the next time I went on a sales meeting. I could also use it to improve the customer service I was giving my current clients. If this prospect wanted certain things, it is safe to figure some of my clients and future prospects would want those services too.

Another rejection led directly to a product innovation. I had approached the vice-president of a small, upscale grocery chain. We did a free evaluation for him and then had a meeting together. Frankly, he said, he wasn't impressed with the depth of the report. That was the first time I had heard that objection. He asked if we could amend the form to make it more interactive in testing the employees' product knowledge and friendliness. He also said he would be willing to pay a higher price for that type of report. I went back to my office, added a few more in-depth questions and we had a new form. We charged forty-four percent more for this report because it was more detailed and time consuming. He approved the additions and we were hired. His stores were still a client when I sold the company. Because of his initial rejection I was able to go back and improve our product. I advertised the new form to our grocery clients and several companies jumped at it. Without his objection, I wouldn't have known how to improve the form we were using. It also gave clients another form to use when they had reached their desired results with the most basic shop.

It's great when sales come easily. Obviously, I'll take an easy one over a difficult one any day. In reality, though, no one gets every sale. What is important, though, is that you learn why you didn't get the sale. I tried to analyze every "No" I got to see if I could improve my service or avoid repeating mistakes. Everyone, including companies, goes into slumps. As a wise friend of mine once said, "If you're not moving ahead, you're falling behind."

POINT TO PONDER

• You'll learn the most about your character and your company during the difficult times.

17

Learn from Others' Mistakes

"Fools you are . . . to say you learn by your experience . . . I prefer to profit by others' mistakes and avoid the price of my own." —**Bismarck**

"A man who has made a mistake and doesn't correct it is making another mistake." —**Confucius**

"Those who cannot remember the past are condemned to repeat it." —**George Santayana**

Having made *many* mistakes of my own, I have come to the conclusion that I would rather learn from others' mistakes. If better business people than I have touched the proverbial "hot stove" and gotten burnt, do I too have to burn my hand to learn that it wasn't a good idea? Learning from your mistakes is called experience and experience is good. But I don't want to go through my whole life making mistakes before I learn something. If I know that something didn't work for Henry Ford, Bill Gates, Donald Trump, etc., there's a good chance it won't work for me either. I want to learn from *their* mistakes. You don't get a badge of courage for the number of times you mess things up, so make as few mistakes as possible.

When I first started my company I talked to some business people about what I should do first. They all said, "Write a business plan." Did I? No. I did it the hard way and learned for myself. When you start a company, write a business plan. That was probably my third biggest mistake behind hiring relatives and not delegating work when I had the chance.

WE ALL MAKE MISTAKES

- Henry Ford forgot to put a reverse gear in his first car.
- Thomas Edison once spent more than $2 million on an invention that proved useless.

- Hall of Famer Reggie Jackson struck out more times than anyone else in the history of the game, over 2,500 times.
- "We don't like their sound and guitar music is on the way out." —Decca Recording Company rejecting The Beatles, 1962.
- "That is good sport. But for military, the airplane is useless." —Ferdinand Foch, Commander in Chief, Allied forces on the western front, World War I.
- "The television will never achieve popularity; it takes place in a semi-darkened room and demands continuous attention." —Harvard Professor Chester L. Dawes, 1940.
- "We don't tell you how to coach, so don't tell us how to make shoes." —A large sporting shoe manufacturer to Bill Bowerman, inventor of the "waffle" shoe and co-founder of Nike, Inc.
- "This 'telephone' has too many shortcomings to be seriously considered as a means of communication. The device is inherently of no value to us." —Western Union internal memo in response to Alexander Graham Bell's telephone, 1876.

Mistakes aren't all bad. They do give us the basis for experience and we usually learn a lesson more quickly from a mistake than from someone merely giving us advice. In the long run, though, I'd still rather make fewer of the mistakes myself and learn from others. The less mistakes you make the faster you can move towards your goals. I'm quite willing to learn from someone else's bankruptcy than gain the experience by going through it myself.

POINTS TO PONDER

- The biggest mistake you can make is not learning from your past mistakes.

- The first thing I did when I decided that I wanted to get into speaking as a career was e-mail every speaker on the North Carolina Speaker's Association website and ask them for advice. More than half of them responded, and I had several phone conversations with speakers that let me know some of the important things to be aware of as I was starting out.

18

It's a Numbers Game

"Even if you're on the right track, you'll get run over if you just sit there." —**Will Rogers**

"Everything comes to him who hustles while he waits." —**Thomas Edison**

This chapter has a very important but very basic idea behind it. If you knock on enough doors, some of them will open. When I talk about "your product" in this chapter I will assume it is a quality product that's currently unknown to people.

We'll use mystery shopping as an example. We had a good service that would improve a company's customer service and profits. I personally had the expertise to meet with companies' management and advise them on ways to improve. Great, now where are all the clients lining up to use this great service? The problem was that no one knew we were out there. We hung out the proverbial "shingle" and waited for customers to come to us. I had to tell people we were out there. At that point, it became a numbers game. The more businesses I approached about mystery shopping, the more business I got.

In my talks, I like to use the example of trying to get a date. If I ask one woman out and she says, "No" then I don't have a date for Saturday. She could have any number of reasons for turning me down—she's married, she's focusing on work and school right now, she thinks I'm too ugly. The reason doesn't matter. I asked one woman and she said, "No." Now, if I ask ten women, one is bound to say, "Yes." It doesn't matter that the other nine turned me down. I wanted a date for Saturday and now I have one. (Remember that rejection is part of the game. I could be disappointed that nine out of ten women declined my offer or very happy that one said, "Yes."). Let's say I was very outgoing. Over the course of a couple of months, I ask seventy-five women out. Six or seven are likely to accept. To my friends, I would seem like a real ladies' man because I would always have a date. Meanwhile, there will always be a better looking or more successful man without a date wondering why I date so much. The reason? He never asks. He doesn't let anyone know he is available.

Now let's go back to the mystery shopping example. Once I understood the numbers principle, I used it to keep track of the number of calls I made, the sales letters that were sent out, and the results I achieved. I knew that if I sent out a hundred sales letters, it would yield one or two clients. If I sent out a thousand letters, it would yield between ten and twenty clients. I could multiply the numbers depending on how many letters I was able to send. I did the same thing with phone calls. The important thing is to get out there and make yourself known. Most people will turn you down. It doesn't matter. Just keep going. Don't get disheartened by rejections. If you know going in that fifty phone calls will result in one customer then you should expect forty-nine rejections. Also, remember it's not personal. There will be many legitimate reasons, no matter how great your product, that people will say, "No." Maybe they can't afford it. Maybe they don't have the time. Perhaps they already have a product or service like yours. (When you get more experienced you can come up with standard responses for the most common rejections, such as, "It's too expensive.") For now though, you just have to get in front of people. Getting in front of people could be any number of things depending on your type of business. For me, it was sales letters. It could be networking, cold calling, advertising, public relations, industry conferences, or literally going business to business or house to house and knocking on doors (which I've done).

Many of the examples I use are from a service company, since that's what I did. But "The Numbers Game" applies just the same to retail and the Internet. A great example is Amazon.com. There was a time when you couldn't go thirty seconds without hearing their radio commercial searching for a bigger warehouse to house all their books. They were constantly getting in front of their customers and prospects and telling them, "Here we are." And it worked. There may be better websites that do the exact same thing as Amazon, but I couldn't name them. I don't know that they're out there.

You'll never make it by just waiting for the phone to ring. You must get in front of your prospects, wherever they are. I've found that a little luck can follow you if you're out there trying to make things happen.

"I'm a great believer in luck, and the harder I work the luckier I get."—Stephen Leacock.

I once got a client who overheard me on the phone in a prospect's waiting room. I never got the prospect, but the client was still with us two years later when I sold the company. I once overheard a restaurant owner talking in a client's restaurant. I approached him and was able to get his restaurant as a client, too. Both times luck was involved when I got the client, but I wouldn't have been lucky if I was sitting in my office waiting for clients to come to us.

As your business grows and becomes established, you will still need to get in front of prospects (GM, Sears, and Wal-Mart still advertise everyday), but it will never be more vital than in your early start-up phase. If you don't get enough customers in the beginning you won't be able to get established. It will get a little easier as you go along. Going into our third and fourth years we often picked up clients by referrals and the reputation we were building.

ACTION PLAN

• Track all of your sales efforts in a spreadsheet to find out how many times you must complete each activity to yield one client.

WEEK ENDING	1ST MAILING	2ND MAILING	3RD MAILING	PHONE CALLS MADE	FUTURE	MEETINGS	YES	NO
1/8/00	150	0	0	50	3	0		16
1/15/00	100	150	0	65	4	2	2	19
1/22/00	100	100	150	75	7	3	3	24
1/29/00	75	75	100	50	6	4	5	19
2/5/00	200	100	100	50	8	3	4	24
2/12/00	200	100	75	30	9	4	5	26
2/19/00	250	150	100	75	7	4	8	25
2/26/00	200	125	50	50	13	6	12	32
Totals	1275	800	575	445	57	26	39	185

Total # of mailings	2650
Total # of phone calls	445
Total customer contacts	3095
Number of new clients	39
% new clients to total contacts	1.3%

I had a service business, so this is how my spreadsheet looked. It can also be used for Internet businesses or retail if you substitute what applies to your business. For my business, I often sent prospects several different mailings over time. I also made cold calls and calls to prospects that I had mailed to. I counted each phone call even if I got a secretary or voice mail. The total number of contacts I made to customers was 3095. (Sometimes I would send several mailings and make several phone calls to a prospect. I counted each time I tried to contact a prospect. Rarely will a prospect say, "Yes" on the initial call.) A "future" is a prospect that is interested in the product or service, but isn't ready to buy just yet. "Meetings" were the number of meetings I went to based on my attempts. The "Yes" column was the number of clients we got from the mailings and phone calls. You will notice over time that your numbers in the "Yes" column will increase as your earlier labors start to bear fruit. People who were not initially ready to buy your product will start to call. From my chart I know that I garnered 39 clients from my 3095 contacts. That means for every hundred mailings and phone calls I made, I would attract 1.3 clients. This gives me a basis for growing or maintaining my business. I now know that if I want to double the size of my business I will need to have about 6000 customer contacts because I can expect a success rate of 1.3% in attracting new customers. Knowing these numbers also helps me mentally. If I contact 100 prospects and three buy my product, I haven't been rejected 97 times, I've actually doubled my normal success rate. The success rate might seem low but keep in mind I often had to approach a prospect five, six, or seven times before I got a "Yes" or a "No."

This same process could be used for a retail store. I would take the number of direct mail pieces I sent out. If I advertised I would take the number of estimated people that would see my ad. (The place you advertise should be able to give you an estimate of the number of people that will see your ad.) Get the best estimate of the number of patrons that come into your store. From the register receipts you can get the actual number of paying customers. From these numbers you can determine how many people you have to "get in front of" to get one paying customer.

19

Next!

"Activity is the life blood of a successful selling process. Networking is probably the most effective way of creative activity." —**James Lewin**

Time is everyone's most valuable resource. You can borrow, find, steal, win, or make more money, but we all have only twenty-four hours a day to work with. It's what we do with those hours that determines how successful we'll be. I learned quickly that I couldn't afford to let others waste that time.

What I learned was that *not everyone is a prospect.* I was wasting my valuable time talking and meeting with people who would never buy my product. When I started, I was just happy to get in front of prospects, and I figured they all could become clients. But the more time you spend talking with someone who isn't going to buy your product the less time you have to spend in front of people who will.

A businessperson I know taught me "Next!" He said the sooner you can *disqualify* a prospect the sooner you can find the prospect that will buy. Whether it's a service or a retail business not everyone you come in contact with is a buyer. For example, let's say you own a pet store and two separate customers come in. It's important to know who is the real buyer and who's just looking. So you go to the customer with the small child that's in love with the pug in the window. Too many beginners think, "Little kid. Loves dog. I got this one." But this is where you have to identify the real buyer. They may love the dog, but they could be lousy prospects. One of the most important things is can they afford the product (in this case a dog)? If they can't afford the pug or any similar dogs in your store, it's "Next!" You do it politely and professionally, but there is no sense selling to someone who can't afford to buy your product. You go to the second customer and repeat the process.

The process involves asking qualifying questions. Maybe the family lives in an apartment and can't have pets. "Next!" Maybe they already have a cat and were just looking. "Next!" Perhaps someone in the family has an allergy to dogs so they couldn't have one even if they wanted to. "Next!" Don't run away from the prospect like they're on fire, but if I asked enough questions and found out the prospects were not qualified buyers, I would give them my card and tell them if they needed any assistance to come get me. Then I would go help the next customer.

The same thing goes for networking. It can be useful if you talk to the right people. Very often, though, I see people talking with someone they know or getting caught up in conversations with people that aren't prospects. How do you network if you only talk to people you know? The worst thing is trying to get away from someone who is rambling on about something inane. What do you do? "Next!" I asked my business friend, "Isn't it rude to just cut them off once you know that you're not going to do business?" He explained that you can politely excuse yourself because there are several other people there that you want to speak to before they leave. And, if they don't like it, too bad. You're there to meet people. The same actually applies to people you can do business with. If they want your product or you want theirs, tell them there are several other people you need to see and either set a meeting time or ask when would be good time to call.

Early on, I hired a telemarketing firm to make calls for me. I was too afraid to make them myself. They got me a meeting with a gentleman who ran a two-person café at a courthouse. I quickly realized when I went to the meeting that he was just bored. He had no intention of buying my service, but I went down to his café when it was slow and gave my sales pitch. I followed up several times to no avail. Now, I could disqualify him in the first thirty seconds of our meeting, but back then I sat with him for forty-five minutes. If that happened several times, you could easily see how much time I could waste.

POINTS TO PONDER

- "Next!" doesn't just apply to prospects and potential clients, but to other aspects of business, too. Wouldn't it be good to know that your chances of getting a loan at a particular bank were very slim before you filled out all the paperwork and sent your application fee? What if you could speed up the interviewing process of potential employees by disqualifying them earlier?

- Most people apply "Next!" to their buying decisions. When you go into a bookstore, don't you usually flip through several books only to pick out one or two to purchase? Once you decided a book wasn't right for you, you put it back on the shelf and grabbed another one. "Next!"

20

The Value of Patience

"Prayers of the modern American: 'Dear God, I pray for patience. And I want it **right now.** *"* —**Oren Arnold**

"The key to everything is patience. You get the chicken by hatching the egg—not by smashing it. " —**Arnold Glaslow**

In America, we want instant gratification—the quick, splashy commercial and the ten-second sound bite. Most of us want everything yesterday. With the inception of the Internet, cell phones, fax machines, pagers, etc., we can get information almost as it happens. Our parents' generation had to wait for the morning paper or evening news to find out about breaking news. Today, we have twenty-four hour news channels and the Internet where we can watch events unfold. Patience is not a virtue in the new millennium.

In business though, patience is still and will always be necessary. Most "overnight successes" you hear about actually took years to get where they are. I'm sure you can think of an actor who was a so-called "overnight success." He was in three movies, a television show, and the cover of *People* all within a matter of months. What people don't consider are the years the actor spent studying, working for free in local plays, and going on audition cattle calls before getting his big break. The same thing can be said of an athlete who breaks out seemingly overnight. What you don't hear about is how many years he spent toiling in the minor leagues before getting called up to the majors. There are many similar occurrences that happen in business, and if you lack patience you could very easily give up too quickly.

If I read a story about myself, I would probably think that everything happened very quickly for me. I graduated from college and started and sold my own company within a four-year time span. Believe me, living through those four years sometimes felt more like forty years. What most people don't know about are the days I literally pulled the sheets over my head because I didn't want to get out of bed or played baseball on the computer because I was too afraid to make sales calls. I quit my job, had only one client, and delivered papers to make ends meet before I got my second client. I had some very *long* days with plenty of opportunities to quit. It was patience that helped me through. As hard as it was, I knew that I had a good, viable idea that would eventually work. If I gave myself time, I would eventually make it.

Patience is very difficult to master, but necessary if you want to do things right. When I owned my company, I would often come up with product ideas and want to offer them the next day. Sometimes I did and they proved to be more trouble than they were worth because I didn't properly plan them out. Most things take time to do right and rushing things will only backfire in the long run. The "Last Supper" took four years to paint. What if DaVinci had tried to finish it more quickly? It wouldn't be the timeless classic it is. Four years is a long time to work on a painting, but obviously it was worth it in the end.

I had a similar problem writing this book. I thought I would work day and night writing it, knock out a query letter and proposal, and then wait for responses. My wife was pregnant and I wanted to get everything done before she went into labor. She was my proofreader and once the baby came, I would lose that. Luckily, I resisted the urge to *just get it done.* I knew that if I was going to put my name on the cover, I wanted something of quality. It takes time to do things right. Even the one-page ideas take several rewrites before they are clear and sharply focused. It takes time to write a proper, thorough book proposal. I'm glad that I fought my natural urge to just get it done and move on to the next project.

While doing research for the book, I came across several examples of writers who showed patience and eventually made it. They may inspire you to keep going even when the going gets tough:

- Tom Clancy wrote his first novel, *The Hunt for Red October,* during his spare time while working for his family's insurance agency.
- E. E. Cummings' poetry was rejected more than a dozen times until it was finally published by his mother.
- Stephen King, currently America's most prolific and successful contemporary author, had seven novels rejected before

Carrie was published by Doubleday. He received $200,000 for the book and his wife was asked at a lunch in King's honor what the first major money meant to her and Stephen. She replied, "I hope Steve can stop teaching and concentrate on writing." That's patience.

A second reason patience is so important is because the business world moves *so* slowly. If I had clients who wanted their reports on their desk by Monday morning, it had to get there by Monday! But when I would call on Wednesday to follow up on the reports I'd often be told they hadn't even had a chance to look at them yet. I've had projects where everyone agreed on all the details and it would still take a month or two to finally start the program. Business just moves slowly. I sometimes wonder how we as a species have come this far. Another thing to keep in mind is that if you have a business that will work with the government, multiply your time estimate by two and pray.

Writing this chapter reminds me of an anecdote that I once heard about a stonecutter:

"When nothing seems to help, I go and look at the stonecutter hammering away at his rock perhaps a hundred times without as much as a crack showing on it. Yet at the hundred and first blow it will split in two, and I know it was not that blow that did it, but all that had gone before."

POINTS TO PONDER

- After it took Thomas Edison 2000 tries to invent the light bulb, a young reporter asked him how it felt to fail so many times. "I never failed once," Edison said, "It just happened to be a 2000-step process."

While reviewing this lesson I came across several examples of how well-known stars were patient and stuck with their craft until they finally got their break:

- Suzanne Somers did not become a star until her tenth pilot, *Three's Company*, became a hit.

- John Spencer (*L.A. Law* and *The West Wing*) kicked around for more than a decade as a character actor, and at the age of 32 was back to waiting tables. He waited more than twenty years for his big break.

- Supergroup Loverboy wrote in the jacket of their "Classics" album that "After being turned down by countless labels" they were finally signed by CBS.

ENTREPRENEURIAL TRAINING

Athletes train their bodies by running, lifting weights, and practicing their sport. Entrepreneurs can also do things to sharpen their skills and minds. This section delves into how to keep your creative juices flowing and how to "think out of the box." Consider this next section as a gymnasium for your mind.

21

Dare to Dream

"I have learned this at least by my experiment: that if one advances confidently in the direction of his dreams, and endeavors to live the life which he has imagined, he will meet with success unexpected in common hours." —**Henry David Thoreau**

"If you hear a voice within you saying 'You are not a painter,' then by all means paint . . . and that voice will be silenced." —**Vincent van Gogh**

Another quote I like from Thoreau is, "The mass of men lead lives of quiet desperation." I had a long talk about that thought with my wife one night. Think about all the people you went to high school with and the grand futures they imagined for themselves written in the captions under their yearbook pictures. How many of them ever fulfilled that caption? Not many. Somewhere along the line they forgot their dreams. They played it safe. Maybe they were told their dream was too hard to accomplish. Perhaps they never had it in them to strive for that dream in the first place. They live their lives, but somewhere deep inside their heart of hearts, there is something they longed to do, but didn't. I told myself that I would not lead a life of quiet desperation. I would go for the brass ring and if I failed, I would fail trying. I was not going to punch a clock until it was time for someone to throw dirt on me. And so, I dream.

It doesn't matter if no one believes in your dream. Too many people I've met do nothing but squelch others' dreams. Their lives did not turn out the way they wanted and they hope you fail, too. It's sad, but true. Those who dare to dream, dare to do. The following is a list of dreamers who dared to do, and they come from various backgrounds:

• Bill Gates quit Harvard, started Microsoft, and subsequently became the richest man in America.
• Michael Dell started Dell Computer from his dorm room at the University of Texas in Austin. At age thirty-two he is richer than Bill Gates was at the same age.

- Edwin Land started the Polaroid Company. He was still in college when he started tinkering in his barn. About twenty years later, Land gave the world the first instant camera.
- Fred Smith founded Federal Express. When, in a school paper, he proposed the idea of reliable overnight delivery, he received the following comment from his Yale University management professor, "The concept is interesting and well formed, but in order to earn better than a 'C,' the idea must be feasible."
- Dave Thomas, founder of Wendy's, was a high school dropout. He went back to school in 1993 and received his GED.
- "So we went to Atari and said, 'Hey, we've got this amazing thing, even built with some of your parts, and what do you think about funding us? Or we'll give it to you. We just want to do it. Pay our salary, we'll come work for you.' And they said, 'No.' So then we went to Hewlett-Packard and they said, 'Hey, we don't need you. You haven't got through college yet.'"—Steve Jobs speaking about attempts to get Atari and HP interested in his and Steven Wozniak's personal computer. Jobs and Wozniak founded Apple Computer Company.
- In the early 1960s, Phillip Knight and his college track coach, Bill Bowerman, sold imported sneakers from the trunk of a station wagon with start-up costs totaling $1,000. That company is Nike.
- Tom Monaghan, founder of Domino's Pizza, was also a college dropout. In 1960, with his brother, he bought a small pizzeria for $900 and expanded it according to a simple strategy— locate stores near campuses or Army bases and deliver within half an hour.

I believe it is important to know that there are many dreamers out there and that their successes did not happen overnight. I used to work the graveyard shift for A&P when I was in high school and in college. It was an unglamorous job stocking the shelves, cleaning the floors, and ringing out insomniacs, but I always had in my mind what I wanted to achieve someday. If someone would ask I would tell him or her my plans. Most of the time they were dismissed with an, "Oh really?" or, "Well, then what are you doing working here?" I should note that packing out cans of Juicy Juice at 3:00 AM is about as far away from the business world—the movers and shakers—as I could get. I would often work alone on Sunday nights when the lights are dimmed to conserve energy. I would eat my lunch and pull out all the business sections from the various papers. (This was both thrifty and educational.) I knew that someday people would be reading about me in those papers. Unfortunately, when you share your dreams with others, they often try to shoot them down. They don't want to be reminded of their own failed dreams. I knew if I told a coworker that someday people would write about me, I'd get a comment like, "Well, then what are you doing with that mop in your hand?" But, undaunted, I continued to dream.

I read in a magazine about a little industry called mystery shopping. I thought that with my experience working in a consumer-related industry I could start a company that would evaluate other companies' customer service. I talked it over with my fiancée and best friend, and it was decided that we would start C&S Mystery Shoppers. I was taking my first steps toward my dream of owning my own business. Over the next few months I planned out my business while working for A&P. Unfortunately I didn't always plan well, but that's a different chapter. When I took my two-week vacation for my honeymoon in May of 1996, I never went back. We had only one client, and I had no business experience. I was going to give it my best shot, and if I didn't make it, at least I failed trying and not just sweeping a floor.

With hard work and a little luck, we did make it. On February 4, 1998, the company I founded was on the front page of *The New York Times* business section. A month later I was in *Vogue* magazine. Along the way, I was named to two New Jersey publication's "40 Under 40" lists. In February 1999, *The New York Times* did a half-page personality piece on me. Later that year, I sold my company. I didn't hit a home run, but I got in the game, got my uniform dirty, and next time I'll do better. Another dream I had was to write my own book, which you are now holding in your hands.

Dreaming helps keep you going during the most difficult times. When you read about my company, it seems that everything happened fairly quickly. In less than four years, I started a company, got national attention, and then sold it. In reality, it felt like forty years. I quit my job and spent a lot of time those first few months playing computer baseball. Things were not going well. We went six months before we got our second client. I lacked direction in the beginning, but I did not give up on my dreams. I believed in myself; I just wasn't always sure which way to proceed. Eventually, I did find that direction and my learning curve kept expanding to result in what you are reading now.

As long as I live I can say that I had a dream to own my own business and I did it. And it was successful on top of that. It is so much better than living a life of quiet desperation. I never wanted to be sixty-five, look at my life, and say, "I know I could have done it. I wish I took the chance when I was twenty-four." I can go in many of the stores I used to work and see people I used to work with doing the same job down the same aisles. I can guarantee you that none of them had ". . . to work in the dairy section of a supermarket for forty years" written in the caption under their high school yearbook pictures.

POINTS TO PONDER

- Keep the dream alive. It sounds obvious and like a cliché, but it will be one of the most difficult things to do when the phone isn't ringing, the only mail are bills, and your salary is zero. The dream of what can be may be the only thing that keeps you going when reality looks very gloomy.

- The dream only dies when the dreamer stops dreaming.

22

Live Your Passion

"Great dancers are not great because of their technique; they are great because of their passion."—**Martha Graham**

It should go without saying, but you have to have passion for what you do. As an entrepreneur, you will be putting in long hours probably six, if not seven, days a week. If you go into a business to chase the quick money, you'll quickly burn out. The desire to earn money only drives you so far. Starting a business is an incredible grind. I thought I was fairly well prepared mentally, and it was still harder than I thought it would be.

Make sure you enjoy what you do. I enjoyed mystery shopping. It was rewarding to see companies that we had worked with for months make improvements based on our reports and suggestions. I sincerely felt that the service we provided made our clients better in their businesses. One time we gave an award for the highest scoring Pizza Hut restaurant in the chain for a calendar year. I felt a rush of pride when I walked into that restaurant and saw the plaque hanging on the wall for everyone to see. I felt like our company was making a difference in their business.

Now don't get me wrong. Sure I was looking forward to making money. But if that had been all that I was after, I would have quit rather quickly. Like most start-ups, it took almost a year before I started to receive a paycheck, and even then, it was less than I had been making before I quit my full-time job. It's kind of funny if you think about it. How many people would take a job with half the pay and twice the hours of their current job? Only entrepreneurs. And don't worry about the money. In time, that will come.

POINT TO PONDER

• Do what you like. Do it better than others. The money will come.

23

Be an Idea Mill

"Ideas shape the course of history." —**John Maynard Keynes**

"Crank–a man with a new idea until it succeeds." —**Mark Twain**

"The vast majority of human beings dislike and even actually dread all notions with which they are not familiar . . . Hence it comes about that at their first appearance innovators have . . . always been derided as fools and madmen." —**Aldous Huxley**

When you stop coming up with new ideas, it's time to punch a clock, and join a union. I'm always continuing to think. If I come up with a new idea, I'll ask my wife, "What if we did this or that? No? Well then, how about this?" Most of my ideas are forgotten five minutes after they are brought up, but I keep my mind active, and never stop asking, "Why couldn't we do this?" Sometimes my ideas are silly and sometimes they're serious, but both types of ideas have their own time and place. Somebody came up with the idea for whoopee cushions and the pet rock, and someone had the idea for General Motors and Delta Airlines. To be successful, you only need to think of one really good idea in your life.

I had a job for almost ten years that I could have done in my sleep. Every night was basically the same—stock the shelves, mop the floor, and ring out customers. I would rather come up with and try out a thousand ideas that don't work, than to go back to the existence of punching in and out every night.

I had an idea to open a baseball card hobby shop. I thought about writing a children's book. I called my friend at 2 AM to ask what he thought about collectible cards of famous African-Americans. I tried to start my own mutual fund with money from relatives. I had an idea to start a mystery shopping company. Hey, that one worked!

My wife had an idea of inventing brooms for tall people. She is 5′10″, so when she sweeps she has to bend over, putting pressure on her back. You never know.

Think out of the box. Find new ways to solve old problems. I get very frustrated with people that give the same old tired solutions to problems. What if you're a twenty-year-old and need start-up capital for your business? Any idiot could tell you to get a bank loan, but the bank won't loan a twenty-year-old money. Borrow the money from your parents? Unfortunately, your parents have three other kids and a mortgage and can't afford it. How about borrowing the money from your friends? That's not going to work since all your friends are in high school or college. What this twenty-year-old needs, and all entrepreneurs need, is the ability to look for solutions that are "out of the box" or unconventional.

When I have a problem that requires creative thinking I try to write down *all* the possible solutions to that problem, no matter how far fetched they are. Then I go back over each possibility to see just how feasible each one is. In the previous example, some of the solutions our young friend might try include saving his money for two years and starting the company at the age of twenty-two. Another idea could be to pray. (Like I said, write down all your ideas.) Hey, maybe an "angel" could help? (An "angel," in this case, is a venture capitalist that will lend money to start-ups for a percentage of ownership.) Maybe he could do his own IPO and sell shares of his company in a private offering. I once read about a winemaker putting their prospectus on the back of their labels, figuring who would be more into their company than their customers? Maybe he could go to Vegas and win the money? Too young to gamble. Scratch that one. Maybe he could look for a partner in the business community that would provide the start-up capital while he supplies the idea and does the work? There could be many other ways for our young friend to raise the money, but he would have to be willing to look for unconventional ways.

Here's a real-life example of "thinking out of the box" from my hometown of Asheville, North Carolina. The heating unit of a local pizza parlor/restaurant was broken. The restaurant had been a modest success, but the owner didn't have the $10,000 he needed to fix the unit. Going into October with no heat is not a good prospect. The owner decided to hold a fundraiser with local bands to raise the money. I heard about this on the radio and also read about it in the local paper. He explained that his business was good for the community, and that's why he should have a fundraiser to support it. The local bands got exposure, and he charged ten dollars a head. Now that's creative thinking.

One tip I can give to learn to "think out of the box" is to step out of your "comfort zone" as often as possible. We all have a comfort zone. We all have places we like to go, people we want to talk to, foods we like to eat, music we like to listen to, and that's what we stick to over and over. It's not necessarily a bad thing. You're naturally going to have places, people, and things you feel most comfortable with. I think the problem occurs when you never step out of that zone. If you never leave that area, you never experience anything new. By trying new things, it will give you the ability to see things from someone else's perspective. You will often see old things in a new light. Yes, you will be uncomfortable, but that's part of it. I will often listen to new music or watch a movie I don't think I'll like. I do it because it gives me a new experience and maybe, if I open my mind, I will like it. (One of my wife's favorite movies was one that I forced her to watch with me.) If I don't like it, at least I tried it. I know what it's about. It's not always easy, though. I still don't step out of my comfort zone too often when it comes to food. I'd prefer Italian, please. My wife and I would like to be friendlier with our neighbors. Our comfort zone is "don't make eye contact and run inside." You can slowly step out of your comfort area. We don't have to have a pool party and invite the whole block. Maybe it's just waving to a neighbor as they're pulling out of their driveway. Then next week when they're mowing their lawn, we could walk over and introduce ourselves. Maybe one day we could invite them over for a barbecue. No matter how you do it, never stop trying new things. Never stop trying to stretch the walls of your comfort zones to broaden your horizons.

POINTS TO PONDER

- What would life be like today if some people did not think out of the box? Here are a few examples:

  - The Wright brothers and the airplane
  - Thomas Edison and the electric light and the phonograph
  - Alexander Graham Bell and the telephone

- Johann Gutenberg and the printing press
- Galileo and the discovery that the sun is the center of the universe
- Sir Isaac Newton and the laws of gravity

- Can you think of one thing that you can do each day to stretch the boundaries of your comfort zone?

24

Exercise Your Mind

"Chess is life." —**Bobby Fischer**

It's "Everything—art, science, sport." —**Anatoly Karpov, the twelfth world chess champion, speaking about his game**

In the introduction to this section, I wrote about exercising your body, which many people do. Yet most people never think about keeping their gray matter sharp and healthy. I would imagine that's because the physical aspect is so apparent. If you have a big behind or get winded going up a flight of steps, you know you need to exercise more. In this modern era when so much of the thinking is done for us, we can almost go through life on autopilot. How many times in your day-to-day life are you forced to solve a difficult problem or to think in new ways? Unless you are reprogramming the VCR, probably not often.

One of the best exercises to keep your mind sharp is to play chess. Like a bench press is to your arms, chess is to your mind. Not only is it a thinking person's game, but it also has many similarities to the business world. Your objective is to defeat your opponent, but you win or lose based upon your skill level and not on luck. I like Monopoly, and your goal is to bankrupt the other players, but how well you do is largely dependent on a roll of the dice. Besides, it's just not that exciting to bankrupt a shoe. In chess, the game involves total strategy. What gambit will you open with? How will you react to the moves your opponent (the competition) will make? What position do you want to be in near the end of the game? This would all be similar to information in your business plan. What are the specific tactics you will use to defeat your opponent? This would be similar to your strategy to double sales in five years and your tactics would be the specific things you will do to reach that goal. Unlike a game like checkers, all the pieces are not of equal value. There are pawns (low-level employees), knights, bishops, and rooks (middle managers) and the King and Queen (President and CEO).

How are you going to utilize these pieces in the most effective way? You don't want to waste your most movable piece, the Queen, on capturing the lowest pieces, pawns. Similarly, you wouldn't want your CEO concentrating his or her time on low-priority projects.

Studies on the effects of children and chess have shown that chess improves a child's visual memory, attention span, and spatial-reasoning ability. It also helps kids learn to plan ahead and evaluate alternatives to make the best decisions. If you want further proof to the benefit of chess, most of the last hundred years the Soviet government has taken the game very seriously. In 1924, chess was integrated into the Soviet party's overall plan. They felt that the game brought out mental qualities valuable to a soldier: "boldness, presence of mind, composure, a strong will, and most important, a sense of strategy."

If you are looking for other games or ways to stimulate your mind, try Stratego. It's a strategy game like chess, where two opposing forces square off against each other, but it's easier to play. Do jigsaw puzzles. Do crossword puzzles. Buy a book of Mensa puzzles, which are full of those mind bending questions that keep your gears turning. Whatever you decide to do, make sure that it forces you to think in new ways, makes you concentrate, and is truly challenging.

POINTS TO PONDER

- Watching TV, even if you're watching an educational channel, is not stretching your boundaries.

- Play Scrabble. Study after study has shown that the greater your vocabulary the greater your earning power.

25

Read, Read, Read

"I find that a great part of the information I have was acquired by looking up something and finding something else on the way."
—Franklin P. Adams

"Anyone who stops learning is old, whether at twenty or eighty. Anyone who keeps learning stays young. The greatest thing in life is to keep your mind young." **—Henry Ford**

One of my favorite places to go is the library. I don't want to sound like a public service announcement, but the library can take you to wonderful places and open up a treasure chest of knowledge waiting to be discovered. When I was a kid my parents thought I didn't like to read. Really it was just that they didn't have anything to read that interested me. What finally did interest me was business and the stock market. I would read anything on those subjects that I could get my hands on. I remember reading the *Wall Street Journal* in the back of English class my junior year in high school. I even gave my teacher a stock pick (too bad she didn't buy Merck in the late eighties). I ran into her several years later at a restaurant and she remembered me as the kid who read in the back of her class. The point is, knowledge is power, and I wanted to learn as much about business as I could.

Before I started my company, I went to the library and read every magazine issue of *Entrepreneur* and *Inc.* that they had. The library had about two years of back issues, and I read every one cover to cover. When I finished with one, I would start on the next. Most of the articles did not have much to do with what I would be facing in the following months, but it did help me immensely in several ways. The following are some of the benefits I received from reading:

- I was able to take comfort in the fact that there were many others out there like me, starting their own business, not having much start-up capital, not having much business experience, etc. It is important to know that there are others who are in the same situation you are.

- Reading gave me confidence. After reading all those articles about how someone started a "ten-million-dollar company in their garage with a loan from their dad," I couldn't help but feel inspired.

- I was more prepared for what it was going to be like to start my own company. I read about people who had successful companies, but maxed out their credit cards in the beginning to keep the company afloat. I read about a business owner who waited two years before he took his first paycheck. When my company started off slowly, and the prospects were unsure, I knew that was all part of the start-up process.

- Many times I found that some information I had read about came in handy at a later date. I was a little more prepared for situations because I had read how other companies had dealt with them.

- If you're lucky, sometimes the articles are immediately applicable to whatever situation you are going through at the moment.

- Sometimes you just read entertaining articles. I still remember reading about a person that came up with the idea of a gumball machine for dogs. The dog would put its paw on a lever, shaped like a bone, and a treat would come out. This didn't help me start my business, but I thought that it was a very clever idea.

I like to read books, especially biographies about famous people throughout history. I like to know what made them so different that they are still remembered today. What qualities helped them get ahead in life? I also read about stocks and the stock market. I do invest, but reading about companies teaches me what makes up a financially solid company.

In the past year or so I have begun to read more books that have absolutely nothing to do with business. It sounds cliché, but reading really can take you away to another place. I've found that it's broadened my horizons and helps me get my mind off business.

ACTION PLAN

- Read a book that has nothing to do with business.
- Take $25 and subscribe to *Inc.* and *Entrepreneur.* The cost is nominal and these magazines will give you a wealth of information about starting and running a business.
- When you read business books, take notes. I often check books out of the library, and by keeping a notebook I have a way to reference points that I want to remember in the future.
- Listen to books on tape. If you drive just twenty minutes a day to your office (most people drive more), that would add up to at least three hours a week you spend in the car. Most books on tape are an hour and a half to three hours long, so you could listen to a book a week while you sit in traffic.

26

Listen, Listen, Listen— My #1 Sales Tip

"A single conversation across the table with a wise man is better than ten years' study of books." —**Henry Wadsworth Longfellow**

"Big people monopolize the listening. Small people monopolize the talking." —**David Schwartz, *The Magic of Thinking Big***

"You can't learn anything with your mouth open." —**Edgar Bergen**

Too many people love the sound of their own voice and therefore never stop to listen to others. They pause for air; you say a couple of things that they are not paying attention to, and then they talk more. Take it from a communications major, *hearing is not listening*. An infant has the ability to hear, but listening is a **skill** that needs developing.

The ability to listen will help you everywhere in life, not just in business. Sometimes my wife is amazed at what I remember. I tell her, "You told me once, and I was actually listening." My mother is the best listener I know. Her key is that she doesn't say anything. You could be on the phone with my mom for a half hour and say, "Are you there?" She'll respond, "Yes. I was listening to you." I have another relative who is the exact opposite. I never bother talking with her because it is hard to get a word in edgewise. If you want a simple trick to help you with listening, think of your head as a mechanical device. You can either use your mouth or ears, but you can't use them both at the same time. Whenever one is in use, the other one will automatically shut off.

Listening will help you *tremendously* in the selling process. Let the client do all the work. They will tell you exactly what they want. When I went to a sales meeting I would speak maybe twenty to twenty-five percent of the time. The rest of the time I was listening and taking notes. I asked questions and let the client tell me what was on their mind. Here's an example of how

I spoke as little as possible in meetings and let the client tell me what they wanted.

Me: Why do you think mystery shopping would be good for your company?

Client: When I started we had just one restaurant and now we're up to seven. I can't be everywhere at once like I used to be, and I don't want to either. Plus, if I go to a restaurant, everyone knows me. I can't get an unbiased opinion of the restaurant.

Me: You seem to be doing well. Are you having any customer service problems?

Client: We're not bad, but I think we could be more focused. Some of our staff has been with us for many years and they've started to get a little lax. We also have a lot more competition than in years past. I think with better service we could sell more to each patron that comes in, such as appetizers or a drink.

Me: We can add a question for "suggested selling" to the form. Besides the basics, such as friendliness and cleanliness, what else would you like on the form?

Client: Well, please include "Was the shopper greeted promptly when they entered the restaurant?" I don't want a family of five just standing around without knowing how long the wait will be. The hostess should point out the day's specials when she seats the customers. I also want everyone in uniform, that includes name badge, white shirt, black shoes, and black pants.

Me: How often would you like us to evaluate each restaurant?

Client: Do each one during a weekend dinner when it's busy. We'll see how they do. Do another one for a weekday lunch. Why don't we try an off-hours visit between 2 and 4 PM. We'll see how they do when it's really slow.

That's how most of my meetings went. That type of example works the same whether you're selling a service or appliances. So many salespeople are so eager to tell the customer everything they know that all they do is talk. How many salespeople have you met who put on a dog and pony show? It doesn't matter if it's life insurance or a stereo. The salesman says, "This is what we have, and this is why it's great. Don't like that one? No problem! Let me tell you about this other one." They never bother to ask you what you really want. They hear, "stereo" and go right into their pitch. I was interested in actually getting the sale, so I listened. Whatever the client talked about was what *they* were interested in, not what I was interested in selling them. In the previously mentioned meeting, I would have been taking many notes. The client told me what his concerns were. He helped me write his own evaluation form. He wrote the schedule for me. When I left meetings, most of the time the work was done for me. If my company did a good job on the evaluations, how could the client not like them? He set all the parameters. It will work the same with customers off the street if you plan to open a retail store. Ask them what they want and they'll tell you. (In the above example, I only spoke 22% of the time.)

Listening to your customers can also help you evolve your product line. I met with the vice president of a supermarket chain. We did a free sample of a mystery shop for him at one of his stores. Afterwards, when we met, he said he didn't care for the shop because he thought the form was too simple, but he remembered that I had said we could change the form if the client wanted. Based on our conversation I went back and developed a more difficult and challenging form. He liked the new form and a new product was developed. I now had something for supermarket clients who wanted to further challenge their employees. I was also able to charge forty-four percent more for this mystery shop than the basic shop. I honestly would not have come up with this idea on my own.

Have you heard the expression, "Keep your eyes and ears open?" Well, sometimes it actually works. I was sitting at the bar in a restaurant doing a mystery shop. I overheard the two patrons next to me, and they sounded like they owned or worked at a restaurant. I introduced myself and it turned out one of the men was the owner of a restaurant down the street. He and the manager were there to discuss his restaurant without being interrupted by his employees. I explained who I was and what we did. He seemed interested and asked me to give him a call in a couple of days. His restaurant later became one of our clients. Another time I made an in-person cold call to a corporation in my area. I had stopped by several times but never got past their house phone. This time was no different. I explained who I was and what I did to a secretary but got nowhere. As I was leaving, a man waiting for a meeting said he had overheard me and would like to hire my company. They were a client for two years and were still active when I sold my company.

As a new entrepreneur, listening will probably be a skill you need to develop. Up until now, you probably haven't had to do much true listening. The jobs you've held up to this point probably haven't been critical. When you go out with your friends, how often do you fill in the blanks of what each other is saying? You can get by in life without truly listening, but if you can learn this skill it will help you tremendously, not only in business, but in your personal relationships as well.

One exercise that will automatically make you a better listener is to talk less. When you're starting out, you're eager to show people what you know. Fight the urge to impress everyone with how much you know and let them talk.

The moral of this chapter is simple—keep your antennae up, your ears open, and your mouth shut.

The five most common poor-listening habits are:

- Interruptions
- Fear of not having all the answers
- Believing that you know better than the speaker
- Overreacting
- Pseudolistening

—Anderson, *Great Customer Service on the Telephone*

POINTS TO PONDER

- Listening is not related to intelligence; it is a learned skill.

- "We quickly forget what we hear. After 1 day we forget 46 percent of what we've heard. After 7 days we forget 65 percent of what we've heard. After 14 days we forget 79 percent of what we've heard." —H. F. Spitzer, researcher

- A good exercise to improve your listening skills is to have someone read a newspaper article to you. Afterwards, write down the basic ideas from the article, and see how accurate you were. This exercise forces you to focus and really listen to what the speaker is saying.

27

I Think, Therefore I Am

"A pessimist is one who makes difficulties of his opportunities."
—**Anonymous**

"To believe a thing impossible is to make it so." —**French proverb**

A business acquaintance once told me not to bring my own "headtrash" to meetings. For example, I was twenty-four when I attended my first sales meeting. In my mind, I kept thinking, "I'm too young. I could be this person's son. He won't take me seriously. I'm too inexperienced." The problem with this thinking was that I was the only one thinking it. The person across the table didn't care that I was young. *I was the one who was hung up about it.* He was only concerned about whether or not my service would benefit his company. This potential client did hire us, but if I had spent too much time defending a perceived weakness, I would have missed out on talking about what the client really wanted to hear.

We all have insecurities that only **we** notice. Who hasn't gone on a first date and been petrified about something only they could see? *That pimple on my cheek is the size of a moon base. I can't get those three hairs to stay down.* If you have ever mentioned it, you were probably surprised to learn that your date hadn't even noticed it.

For a new entrepreneur, "headtrash" could be many things: you're worried that you're too young or inexperienced; you don't have enough capital or connections; you're too small to compete with your competitors; you don't have the right education, etc. The list could go on and on.

One of the biggest problems with headtrash is that if you look hard enough, you'll eventually find something to validate your concern. This will lead you to focus on it even more, creating a vicious cycle. You can begin to blame any failures on this perceived weakness, which only makes it harder to let go. Unfortunately there will always be racism and sexism in the world, but that is an unavoidable, sad fact of life. There are people out there who will not hire someone because of the color of their skin (and that could be *any* color) or what gender they are. I think, however, that there are not enough of these small-minded people to affect the success of your business. Most people can put aside their personal prejudices for money. If you can make or save them money, you can have green skin and come from Venus and they will overlook it. Plus, you never know the types of prejudices a person that you encounter may have. There are people who don't like short people, fat people, bald people, etc. There is no way for you to anticipate the prejudices of people you will meet, so leave your headtrash at home. So far, I have only encountered one person where I thought, "This guy is sexist."

In reality, I had the concern about being too young and inexperienced during the first year and a half of my business. Luckily, I did not voice that feeling in meetings. I could have tried to head off my clients' concerns about my age by saying, "I know I'm young . . . ," or "We are just a start-up . . . ," and then tried to defend a position that was never in question. In the beginning, our first client was Pizza Hut. Several months later we got two more clients—a supermarket chain and a bagel chain. Neither of them asked about my age or how much experience we had. The supermarket client just *assumed* we had worked with other supermarkets. If I had allowed my headtrash about being too young and inexperienced to become an issue, *I could have brought out that concern in them.* It would have been a self-fulfilling prophecy. Had I told the supermarket rep, who had assumed we were bigger than we were, that they would only be our second client, there is a good chance that she would have reconsidered. I know I would be more hesitant to hire someone with only limited experience. She might wonder, "How do I know if they'll be in business in a year? What if they don't have enough shoppers to cover the territory?" If I had brought up these questions to try to ease her mind, I might have lost this client. *They were only concerns in my mind, not hers.* If she had turned us down, I could rationalize it by saying, "I guess I am too young and inexperienced." We did not get the Pizza Hut contract by a large margin, and if I had brought up the (perceived) age issue, it may have cost us our chance to work with them. That would be two clients I could have talked out of hiring us. I met the bagel client, and they wanted to know what other food chains we had worked with. In real life, I told them

Pizza Hut, which was good enough for them. In my example, I would have had no other clients, so they could have said, "No." I would have been 0 for 3 and I started thinking, "I knew everyone would hold my inexperience against me." Someday, I would have looked back and told a co-worker that, "Yeah, I tried to start a business once, but people just didn't want to deal with a young entrepreneur," when in reality, prejudice was where I wanted to find it.

To sum it up, if you have the idea for a company and work hard, more than likely you will succeed regardless of the color of your skin, your gender, your age, or where you went to school.

ACTION PLAN

- A good exercise is to list *how you think others perceive you.* Then ask people that know you to describe how *they* see you. Finally, compare both lists. You might be surprised to find out that how you view yourself is not how others view you. For example, you might think you're too young and inexperienced, while someone else might be impressed by your ambition.

28

Go Outside and Play

"Increased means and increased leisure are the two civilizers of man."
—Benjamin Disraeli

"The end of labor is to leisure." **—Aristotle**

Sometimes you have to shut off the computer and the cell phone and go outside and play. As entrepreneurs we so often throw ourselves into our work so much that we forget everything else. Too many of us wear our workdays as a badge of honor. "I put in sixteen hours a day. Look how hard I work." We also feel that our business needs us so much we can't take any time off. Unless you run a one-man hot dog stand, you can take some time off. I'm not trying to convince you to take two weeks off on a cruise ship, but occasionally we have to step back and do something fun that is **not** work related.

I learned this point the hard way. I got into a serious rut from too many consecutive sixteen-hour days. My mind had turned to oatmeal. I had trouble focusing on what I was doing. Reports that normally took fifteen minutes were taking forty-five minutes. I moped around the office feeling obligated to put in another long day. As much as entrepreneurs sometimes hate to admit it, we're only human. If you left a machine running constantly, seven days a week, it would eventually start to wear out. It's the same with our bodies and minds.

My wife finally convinced me to take some time off. I went to visit my parents in North Carolina for three days. I didn't do much while I was there. I caught a baseball game and rented a few movies. I came back refocused and recharged. All I needed was three days of letting my mind and body relax to get me back on track. My company survived. Later in the year we sent my wife down to North Carolina to recharge her batteries. Again, the company survived.

I now make a conscious effort to fit things I enjoy into my schedule. One thing I love to do is go to movies. No matter how bad a movie is, I forget everything else for those two hours. I also enjoy catching a ballgame. It really doesn't matter what you like to do, just make sure you find time to do it. If you can't find a couple of hours to do the things you enjoy outside of work, what's the point of life?

As an entrepreneur, I know how you feel. You have fifty ideas and you want to get them all done yesterday. I often feel like that, but sometimes you will have to stifle those feelings before you become overwhelmed. Believe it or not, you eventually will be able to find a balance between work and personal life. If you make a conscious effort to work on your personal life, you'll be surprised. You'll be happier and you will be able to get more done in your business life.

ACTION PLAN

- When you're finished reading this page, write a list of everything fun you would like to do in the next year. Then take ten of those items and work them into your schedule just as you would a business meeting. (If your list doesn't have ten things, you need to get a hobby.)
- Make plans for this Friday. Do not work past 4:30 PM. See a movie. Go out to eat. Go to a ballgame. Do something fun.

DEALING WITH PEOPLE

How you deal with people is essential to long-term business success. Not only will you be dealing with different personality types, but with people who all have their own agendas: customers, prospects, employees, vendors, competitors. Last and most importantly, as an entrepreneur, you will have to find a balance between your home and business life.

29

What Did They Say? Be an Effective Communicator

"You can have brilliant ideas, but if you can't get them across, your ideas won't get you anywhere." —**Lee Iacocca**

"I'll pay more for a man's ability to express himself than for any other quality he might possess." —**Charles Schwab**

I must admit that I was a Communications major at Rutgers University because I didn't have the grades to get into the Business School. Besides, in what other college subject can you write about *Star Trek* and *The Simpsons* on a final exam and get full credit? (The class was "Popular Culture in America.") It wasn't until I got into the business world that I realized just how important effective communication is and just how few people are good at it. Looking at it now, it's no surprise that most of the CEOs and business owners I meet have a strong command of the English language and are sharp in their writing and speaking skills.

GET TO THE POINT

Effective communication is making a clear point in the least amount of time. The compliment that I have most often received on this book is that it is easy to read, makes its point, and goes on to the next lesson. Have you ever had someone try to tell you a story and you felt like saying, "Just get to the point!"? I spoke at a university one day and a student wanted to pitch me his business idea. I had car trouble and he helped me out, so I figured it would at least be polite to listen to his idea. We went for lunch and after an hour he still wasn't able to really explain his business idea to me. Was it something as complex as mapping the human gene? Was it something very technical that required a certain background to fully understand? No, it was multi-level marketing over the Internet. He had obviously never heard of an *elevator pitch*.

An "elevator pitch"—and I've heard it called other things—is what it sounds like. You have enough time from when the elevator leaves the first floor and arrives at its destination to make your pitch. This could be literally thirty seconds. You have to have made a concise, coherent point before the person your pitching to gets off the elevator. Many new entrepreneurs don't realize that sometimes all you get is a minute or two in front of a prospect. A busy executive or banker doesn't have time to waste on trying to figure out what you're saying. The same works in retail. We often bring my daughter, age two, shopping. She doesn't sit there for long, if at all. A salesman can't go into a long-winded pitch while one of us is struggling to contain this Tasmanian devil in a diaper.

The same concept applies to writing. Don't try to impress people with your flowery prose—just tell them what you want to tell them. In college, it was always better to write more. I'm reminded of a scene in the movie *Back to School* with Rodney Dangerfield. One of his employees does Rodney's term paper and hands it to him. Rodney's says, "Feels like a C. Why don't you bulk it up and add a few graphs." In business, it's the exact opposite. I spoke with one executive who said that his old boss required one-page proposals or less. If it went over one page, no matter what the subject, it was thrown in the garbage. You might love your writing style, and be impressed with the seven-page proposal you've just written, but it's unlikely to get read. People are too busy. At most, they'll skim through it looking for the important points and ignore the rest. Here's a good example of effective, concise, to-the-point writing. We've all gone to the video store and read the back of the box to see what the movie's about. In a few paragraphs, the writer has condensed the basics of a two-hour movie. How many times have you said, "Sounds interesting. Let's get this one"? If they had a two-page summary on the movie, would you have read it? Of course not.

MESSAGE SENT IS NOT ALWAYS MESSAGE RECEIVED

Have you ever told somebody to do something you thought was very simple and they did something else? What most people don't realize is that the message sent by you is not always the message received by the other individual. (There are other parts of the equation such as the medium and feedback, but I'm not going to discuss those. For example, your cell phone dies during the conversation so the message was disrupted.) I saw a funny example of this in the television show *Dr. Katz*. One of the doctor's patients was talking about his experience when he first went away to college and his roommate asked him if he wanted to split a pie. He thought it was an odd request because to him a pie meant something like an apple pie, but he reluctantly agreed because he wanted to fit in. It was funny for my wife and I because in the Northeast, when someone asks you if you want to split a pie, everyone knows they mean a pizza. When you are trying to communicate, you have to think about the other person's background. They may not have what you think are common points of reference. To me, a "Yankee" is a member of my favorite baseball team. To a Southerner, a "Yankee" is someone from the North. To a European, a "Yankee" is an American. Depending upon the person's background, they could have a totally different meaning for the word "Yankee." If my wife says that she hates the "Yankees" she means the baseball team. If she's talking to a neighbor in North Carolina, they might think she hates Northerners. The message she has sent might not be received the way she intended.

ADAPT YOUR COMMUNICATION STYLE

It is very important to be able to adapt your communication style to match that of the person you are speaking or writing to. It's your job to make them feel comfortable and people feel most comfortable with people that are like them. For example, I met with a business owner to sell him one of my workshops. For the first two minutes he didn't even look at me, and then periodically he'd look up as he was flipping through my workbook. I quickly realized that this gentleman didn't want to hear my whole pitch; he just wanted the basics about how my workshop would help his employees. I felt a little uncomfortable with him, but I adjusted my style, dropped the longer pitch, and told him what he wanted to know. He said, "Yes." Needless to say, it wasn't a long meeting. The next day I met with another business owner. We spoke for about an hour and a half. He told me about his kids, his views on today's workers, and his time in the war. Did I need to know all of this? Of course not, but that was his style. He's a very nice gentlemen and a people person. He wants to know the people he's working with, so I slowed down my delivery and listened to his stories. He also said, "Yes."

You have to communicate with people in the medium they feel most comfortable. Face to face is always best, at least initially, but it is not always possible. I ask people, "Do you use e-mail?" They may have an address within the company, but some people loathe to use it. Other people couldn't live without it and would much rather receive an e-mail than a phone call. It doesn't matter to me—whatever makes them feel comfortable.

USE COMMON, EVERYDAY LANGUAGE AND EXAMPLES

When I communicate I try to use simple vocabulary and everyday examples. When I wrote about going to the video store and reading the back of the box, everyone can relate to that. I sometimes take the *Reader's Digest* vocabulary quiz and I always score very high on it. I could utilize my sizable phraseology to dazzle numerous, divergent audiences. Translation: I could use the big words I know to impress people I meet. Which is more impressive? The first sentence. Which is the one everyone would understand and relate to? The second sentence. I also use self-deprecating humor. People don't like it when you take yourself too seriously. *Appropriate* humor can help put people at ease. For example, in my workshop on goal setting I tell the audience that one of my goals is for physical fitness. Then with a big smile I say, "It's hard to look this good." That always gets a laugh. I then say that I'm not sure if they're laughing at me or with me, but at least their happy. One thing to remember when using humor is that it can be very effective, but don't forget that you are a businessperson and not Jerry Seinfeld.

LEARN TO SPEAK IN PUBLIC

By "learn to speak in public," I'm not talking about being a professional public speaker, but simply learning to speak in front of a group. Many studies have shown that Americans' number one fear is public speaking. I find it hard to believe that death is a viable alternative to speaking in front of a group of people, but many seem to think so. Speaking can help your career and business immensely. You might have to pitch your idea for fifteen minutes to a room full of business people. You might have to address a local business organization, like the chamber of commerce, to increase your credibility.

As a business owner, communication will be essential to your survival since you will constantly be communicating with customers, prospects, vendors, employees, bankers, other local businesses, and competitors. The better you communicate, the better your chance not only of survival, but of long-term success.

POINTS TO PONDER

- Have your pitch thought out ahead of time. Most people who are effective at giving a brief pitch or introduction of themselves have one written down and rehearsed. When I ask a prospect for a brief meeting to introduce my seminars, I know exactly what I'm going to say. I often use the same examples and jokes in several meetings.

- If you want to write sharper or more clearly, think of it as if you were writing a classified ad and being charged for every word. If you got a bill at the end, you would figure out how to write it more effectively.

- Here are four quick tips about speaking in front of an audience.
    1. Since so many people fear speaking in front of others, you already have some of their respect by even going in front of them.
    2. Your audience wants to see you do well. No one wants to sit there for an hour and see someone bomb.
    3. When you make a mistake or forget something you wanted to say, you're the only one who knows it. The audience hasn't heard your material and won't realize you forgot a minor point.
    4. The audience doesn't expect you to be perfect. I was doing a workshop recently and completely drew a blank. I shared with the audience that I'd just forgotten my next point, and someone jokingly said that that's what happens when you turn thirty. I went along with the joke, and then went on with my talk.

30

Attend the School of Hard Knocks

"It is all one to me if a man comes from Sing Sing or Harvard. We hire the man, not his history." —**Henry Ford**

"Fortunately for us, Japan is opening its first business school in the near future. This is likely to produce a measurable drop in Japanese productivity." —**Felix Rohatyn, investment banker**

Father to son: "These days, education is all important. Either you have to go to college, or start your own business so that you can hire people who did." —**Joe Griffith,** *Speaker's Library of Business*

"I have a degree in architecture, but I've never used it except as a bookmark or a drink coaster." —**Weird Al Yankovic**

I think education is important, but it is vastly overrated in our society. I graduated high school in 1989, and it seemed that everyone was going to college, whether or not they were really qualified. Obviously if you're going into certain professions, such as medicine or law, higher education is necessary. But, when it comes to starting your own business, you can definitely succeed without going to college. One of the easiest ways to succeed is by possessing something much more useful than a college degree—common sense. Now don't get me wrong—you can get a wonderful education at a top business school, but there is only so much you can learn in a classroom. There are many more things, however, that can't be taught. In business school, you can learn about balance sheets, cash flow, return on investment, etc., but you're not going to *learn how to get that cash flow* and other *practical* applications.

I think about all those students out there who owe $50,000 or more in student loans. That amount of money could be the start-up capital for their company. I had about $2,500 in start-up capital when I started my company, so $50,000 would have really helped out. It's true that some of the mistakes I made could have been avoided if I was a business major (such as *not* having a better business plan). But there are many other lessons that I learned only by going through the grind. I don't think that most textbooks will tell you to, "Watch Out for Number One." They are not going to teach you how to deal with rejection when potential customers or investors don't like your ideas or products.

Only those that have MBAs from Harvard or Wharton advertise it. I don't know where my clients went to school. I don't know if they even got past the sixth grade. All I knew was that they owned six supermarkets or two Wendy's and wanted to use my service. Where did I go to school? I think over the years it only came up twice in casual conversation. What about grades? No one knows how I did in school. Did I graduate first or last in my class? It doesn't matter. All clients care about is what you can do for their company.

College can have a tendency to dull your sharpness. College life is structured. You can schedule yourself off on Friday or for classes not to start until 11:00 AM. If you hand a paper in late, you can appeal to the teacher to not deduct late points. The business world doesn't work that way. People are always running and if you're not running too, they pass you right by. Hand in a proposal a week late, and somebody else will have already beaten you out. If you go to school and want to get a better idea what the outside world is like, commute one semester and take all morning classes. After getting up at 6:00 AM, fighting traffic, bad weather, and searching for a parking spot, you'll get a taste of the real world.

I'm not totally against college. I have a degree myself. College can be a wonderful learning experience if you don't party it away, but it's just one way to learn. If you're not sure what you want to do with your life and you have a scholarship to State U., go. I just don't think college is the *only* avenue you have to take.

Many famous and ultra-successful business people never got their college degree. Bill Gates dropped out of Harvard. Michael Dell dropped out of the University of Texas. Dave Thomas (Wendy's) never went to college and was a high school dropout (he went back to school in 1993 to get his GED). Tom Monaghan quit college and founded Domino's Pizza. Andrew Carnegie stopped formal schooling at the age of thirteen and took a job in a cotton factory for a $1.20 a week. He would later found Carnegie Steel Co. and at one point was the richest man in the world. If you have the idea, don't wait. Go out there and do it.

POINTS TO PONDER

- It's not where you start that matters, it's where you end up. Many of the schools where I speak at would not have accepted me as a student out of high school.

- Albert Einstein did poorly in math at school, and he didn't begin to speak more than single words until about the age of four (the average age is two).

- Ross Perot graduated 454th in his class of 925 at the Naval Academy. When he did recruiting for his company he went to tiny St. Mary's College on the plains in western Kansas because he felt they were hungrier than MBAs from Harvard.

- General George Custer graduated last in his class at West Point in 1861.

31

Love Your Family, but Don't Work with Them (my biggest mistake)

"If you pick the right people and give them the opportunity to spread their wings—and put compensation as the carrier behind them—you almost don't have to manage them." —**Jack Welch, General Electric**

Unless your cousin is Bill Gates or Michael Dell, don't hire your relatives. It sounds simple but it was one of the biggest, if not *the* biggest, mistake I made in starting my business. It is a very easy trap to fall into and a very difficult one to get out of. I have seen marriages break up because of it and relationships strained. Working with relatives is a problem waiting to happen. For every set of brothers that go on to found the famous XYZ Corporation, there are a hundred that stop speaking to each other. It can be done, but it is very difficult and it can cause damage to the relationship far beyond the life of the business.

I started my little mystery shopping business in a spare room like so many other companies have begun. We had only one client, but once I got the hang of things business started to pick up. The business grew and we moved my office into the master bedroom. This was decision time. My wife had helped with the business, but I did the bulk of the work. Now things were too much for one person. My wife quit her job and joined C&S full time. It was a mistake both of us would regret.

I figured, my wife is intelligent and she's cheap labor. She won't ask for time off, vacations, or sick days. She has everything to lose or gain (just as I did) so she will be focused. The mistake was that my wife is not a businessperson. She is a great person, but horrible at business. She is a worker, not a manager. Since it was just the two of us, I was asking her to do things that were beyond her capabilities. She never got better at those things and started to resent the business. These two factors led to some big fights. Luckily, we had enough love and communication that we prevented us from speed dialing a divorce lawyer. Each day, though, as the mistakes and resentment mounted, it took less to set us off. I resented that she could not get better at her job, and she resented that the business was consuming our life. These fights were also affecting the business. Since my wife could not implement certain strategies I was trying to develop as we grew, it dramatically slowed down our potential growth. We did eventually move into an outside office, and we both looked forward to not seeing each other as much. Thankfully, the story does have a happy ending.

The same rule applies for all relatives, not just spouses. I've worked with my brother, sister, mother, father, mother-in-law, sister-in-law, and best friend, not because they were qualified, but because they would work for free (or very little). Don't get me wrong, I love them all, but at one time or another they all made mistakes causing me to want to wring their necks. Since they were family what could I do? Am I going to yell at my mom who was working for free? One time my brother evaluated the wrong restaurant. He felt bad, but what was I going to say? He is my daughter's godfather. If they were employees, I could reprimand them or fire them. As relatives, all I could do was fix their mistakes and move on. I knew they were all trying to be helpful, but at times it was very frustrating.

You could also run into a problem with freeloading relatives. I was lucky. My family didn't mind working. But what happens if you hire your brother-in-law to be your restaurant manager and he turns out to be a stiff? It's very easy for a business owner to get taken advantage of. The relative could say, "He won't fire me, I'm his brother, cousin, niece, etc." What if there is impropriety? What if you're brother-in-law is skimming from the register or taking steaks out of the freezer? Do you call the police on your sister's husband? What reason do you tell your sister for firing her husband? Do you keep him on and tell him to never do it again? It's a hassle any business owner doesn't need. And won't the holidays be fun!

My wife and I agreed not to make this same mistake twice. For my new business, if I need help, I will put an ad in the newspaper and interview people. My wife is very happy being a wife and mother. I am happy being a husband who can tell his wife about his job. As far as my family goes, thankfully, we are all still very close.

The bottom line is that no business is worth coming between you and your loved ones. I knew one business owner who told his wife to choose between working in their business or divorce. He is now divorced and later sold the business, so now he has neither.

POINTS TO PONDER

- Businesses and business relationships don't always work out. If you choose to work with a relative or friend, you have to be prepared that the business could someday come between you.

- If you do hire a relative, are you hiring them for the right reasons? Are they qualified to do the job you're asking of them? How accountable will they be to you? What happens if they don't work out as an employee?

- Even if you're not married now, ninety percent of American eventually do marry, and your spouse will have a large say in your entrepreneurial ventures. Will your spouse put up with your sixty to seventy hour work weeks? Does your spouse want the security of a weekly paycheck and health benefits instead of the unpredictable life of an entrepreneur? What about children? This is an especially important issue for female entrepreneurs. Do you want to work sixty hours a week while you're eight months pregnant? Will your husband watch the children while you go back to work?

32

Win Friends and Influence People: Learn People Skills

"Vanity is so secure in the heart of man that everyone wants to be admired; even I who write this, and you who read this." —**Blaise Pascal (1623–1662)**

"He who refuses praise the first time that it is offered does so because he would hear it a second time." —**Duc de La Rochefoucauld**

I borrowed the title for this chapter from the best selling work by Dale Carnegie, *How to Win Friends and Influence People*. It was first published in 1937, but is just as relevant today. Unfortunately, this was not a concept I grasped with my first business, and it wasn't until I started my speaking career that I realized what it could do for my business and my life.

People skills are so important because you will depend on other people to help make your business successful. As long as you have your business, you will need the help of employees, customers, vendors, bankers, your friends and family, and the community to keep your business going. I used to think that being smarter or being right was enough. I felt that if I had the better plan, wouldn't it be obvious to everyone? What I didn't realize what that not everyone has the same intelligence, the same way of solving a problem, the same viewpoints, or the same agenda.

I'm sure you know people who bully their way through life. When you know they are on the phone you think, "Now what?" You also know people who can give you constructive criticism in a way that makes you feel better about yourself. People skills are about making other people feel good about themselves and not about boosting your own ego.

Even if you don't do business with someone, you want to leave them on good terms. I've had several instances where I wanted to tell someone off or at least send them a strongly-worded letter, but luckily good judgment got in the way. In the end, what would it gain me? Nothing but a lot of burnt bridges. In Chapter 6, I wrote about how I felt after meeting with a particular company president. At that moment, it would have been easy for me to tell him what I really thought of how he ran his company, but what would I have gained? In the short term, it would have felt good to unload, but I might have lost them as a client. At the very least, it would have greatly strained the relationship between our two companies. My people skills have improved much since that meeting. Incidentally, as I write this I am talking with their company about doing a workshop for their managers.

This leads me to my next point—you never know who knows whom. I met with the CEO of a multibillion dollar company in Central New Jersey to discuss one of my workshops. About two weeks later I gave a workshop in Baltimore and mentioned that I met the CEO as an example for a point I was making. I did not give his name. A gentleman came up to me on a break and mentioned that he knew the person I had met with. A week later I met with the VP of another New Jersey company and mentioned that I met with this CEO. (They are in the same industry). The gentleman I was meeting with stated that he not only used to work with this CEO, but also had lunch with him on a regular basis. This can help you open doors or quickly give you a reputation of someone not to do business with.

If you want to leave a good impression, a little flattery never hurts. There are two types of people that like flattery—men and women. Sincere flattery will open many doors for you. I received an e-mail requesting a phone conversation to discuss my opinions on the mystery shopping industry from a woman who was thinking about starting her own business. She started her e-mail with, "I hope that all is well. I read *Business Lessons* as part of an MBA class. I was very impressed with your insights." Someone who read my book and liked it . . . well, sure you can call me. We spoke for about a half hour, and I answered all of her questions. You can catch more flies with honey than with vinegar.

POINTS TO PONDER

- One way to win people over and get them to open up is to talk about their favorite subject—themselves. Would you rather talk about my vacation or yours? My pet or yours? My business or yours? Even when the topic annoys them they'd still rather talk about their situation. For example, if someone doesn't like their dog, they'll still take ten minutes to tell you how it barks at night and eats their slippers. It's hard not to like someone who shows a genuine interest in what we do.

- If you are having a problem with someone, change your approach on how to handle them. For example, a friend was having a problem with his roommate's lack of cleaning. He would criticize the roommate for not helping out, but nothing ever changed. I suggested that instead of pointing out everything he does wrong, try complimenting him on what he does right, even if it doesn't seem like a big deal. The people skills worked. Although his roommate is no Mr. Clean, he does do more to help out, and they both feel better about the lack of criticism.

33

Don't Skimp on Consultants

"Accepting good advice increases one's own ability."—**Johann Wolfgang von Goethe**

Good advice doesn't come cheap. "A business type who was trying to arrange a personnel seminar said that he kept reading reports by psychologists who maintain that people seek other rewards besides money. He said, 'That may be true, but I haven't been able to get those same psychologists to talk about those theories at my management seminar for less than $1,000 plus expenses.'"—**Joe Griffith**

In business I would be what is called a bootstrapper. I never spend a dollar if I don't have to. Bootstrappers are those people you see featured in business articles such as, "Great companies started for under $1,000." I have no problem picking up a filing cabinet at a flea market or an office chair at a "going out of business" sale. In my business I don't have clients visit my office, so I don't care if my office furniture doesn't match, as long as it's functional.

I did, however, find one area where it pays to spend a little more—professional advice. Several times I went with the cheapest professional help I could find and all I got was poor results. I hired a public relations consultant who worked part time out of her home. She seemed nice and professional and at $50 per hour, she was very affordable. Most PR firms I contacted were looking for clients spending several thousand dollars right from the start. I thought finding this consultant was great. Without any PR experience myself, I had gotten my company in *The New York Times, Vogue,* and several local newspapers. I thought that if I hired a professional, it would save me the time of writing press releases, calling editors, etc. A pro would know exactly what to write, whom to contact, and how to do things the right way. I thought I was set. What I soon realized was that I was paying for someone doing PR part time out of her home. When we spoke for the last time about how things were going nowhere, I was in the middle of getting interviewed for my second *New York Times* article. It was a feature in the Sunday section on me, the result of other PR I had worked on and received before I had hired her. That's when I realized that I got what I paid for. Through my own efforts, I received several national write-ups, but the person I hired for PR never even got us into the local newspaper. I went cheap and in the end got no results.

I also had a similar experience with our first accountant. He was nice and I met him through a business association. What I liked most about him, though, was that he was cheap. This was my first experience with the idea that sometimes things are cheap for a reason. When I went to his office for a scheduled meeting to review my year-end taxes, he was still finishing the paperwork as I sat there. My company wasn't that busy in the beginning so I waited, but I was thinking, "What if I had three other meetings today?" This work should have been done long before I ever walked in the door. It's just another case of "you get what you pay for."

I'm not suggesting that you always go with the highest priced professional, but if the average lawyer charges $150 per hour and you meet one that charges $80, you have to ask, "Why?" By paying for good help up front, you will come out ahead in the long run. Take the example of PR. If you have to pay more for qualified PR help, but it leads to greater sales, then the added expense was worth it. The same is true for an accountant that may cost more, but can save you a lot of money at tax time. In the end, you get what you pay for.

POINT TO PONDER

- When hiring professional help, get references that you can check. Would that person recommend them without hesitation? Don't be afraid to question the professional you are thinking of hiring? Whether it's a lawyer, accountant, PR person, or another type of professional, find out how much experience they have in dealing with a company like yours.

34

No One Knows It All

"A man may be so much of everything that he is nothing of anything."
—**Samuel Johnson**

"It is not best that we should all think alike: it is difference of opinion, which makes horse races." —**Mark Twain**

"Compulsory unification of opinion achieves only the unanimity of the graveyard." —**Justice Robert Jackson**

We all know people who are experts at everything, which tells me that they are masters of nothing. You have to have confidence to start your own company. Sometimes that translates to having a big ego. I admit I sometimes have an ego, but I think I am able to keep it in check most of the time. The problem that entrepreneurs run into with confidence or ego is that we feel we can do it all. We say to ourselves, "It's my company and I'm smart enough to do the accounting, planning, etc." That's the kind of thinking that gets people into trouble. Few people are experts in anything, let alone experts in everything. As smart as you are, there is always someone who knows more. Bill Gates has advisors. Ted Turner has advisors. President Bush has a Cabinet. Coaches have assistant coaches. It's okay *not* to know everything. No one will think any less of you.

It is also important to have people around you that have different opinions and ideas than your own. The problem is that most of us are surrounded by people we like, and usually we like people who think the same as we do. In my situation, I would try to bounce ideas off my friends and family and I would usually get, "Sounds good" or "I really don't know." They either didn't know enough about business or thought too much the same as I did. I had no one to bounce ideas off of. If I had a major decision, I had hired consultants I would ask. But that gets expensive and you can't ask them about *every* question and idea you have. You and I need people

157

around us that are not afraid to tell us when we are making a mistake. Different people who will challenge your ideas and look at situations with a different set of eyes are invaluable in your business development.

It's harder than you think to get people to criticize you. I literally begged people who read chapters of this book to criticize it, pick it apart, tell me where I could improve. To me, a good friend or advisor will tell me if I look bad before I go to the meeting. They will tell me my idea won't work before I sink thousands of dollars into it. They will point out if I was too hard on an employee or unfair with a client. A critical friend or advisor is worth their weight in gold. No one is perfect and you should expect to make mistakes. Don't take criticisms as a personal attack but as a way to improve. I'd rather have a friend tell me that my public speaking skills need polishing than to hear about it from a client.

If you're just starting out, try to find a mentor or a peer group. One way to do this is to start networking. Your local chamber of commerce should sponsor regular networking events in your area. Rarely will you have to be a member of the chamber to attend. Another way to meet people is to join an association for your industry or business. Maybe your school has an alumni association. No matter how obscure your business, there will almost certainly be an organization or group you can join. You can also check out your local SCORE group. SCORE is short for Service Corp of Retired Executives. I met with them before I started my company to get their opinions on the direction I was going to take. It is a free service.

By meeting new people in and out of your field you will broaden your horizons and you'll probably learn a lot along the way. You might own a plumbing service, but that lawyer you met at a chamber of commerce function might be useful to you six months down the road.

ACTION PLAN

- Find out where the people you want to meet congregate. Is it the local chamber of commerce, the industry association, or some other organization?

- Before joining an organization or association, find out what you're getting for your money. I've been approached by many organizations that wanted several hundreds of dollars a year to join, and I felt that I would get very little of value in return.

35

Your Worth as a Person Is Not Equal to Your Success or Failure in Business

"The noblest question in the world is, 'What good may I do in it?'"
—Ben Franklin

"All those young people who have a full life ahead of them should be noble and generous so that no matter how small or large one's sphere of influence may be, when one's life is concluded he will have left a great deal of generosity and tenderness behind."—**Dorothy Fuldheim**

It is fitting to end the book with this lesson: As you embark on your entrepreneurial ventures you may or may not be successful in the "profit and loss" sense of business, but being good in business and having a fulfilling life are two distinct things. You can have both, but they don't necessarily go hand in hand. We live in a society that worships celebrities. People are idolized for hitting a ball or acting in a movie. Some rich entrepreneurs and business people are given star status for the wealth they've accumulated. Accumulating wealth is one trait, being a good person is another. That is not to say that there aren't fantastic human beings who were also great business people, but wealth and fame are not synonymous with being a good person. How many times have you seen someone who has a good public persona only to find out more about their lives in a tabloid scandal?

Not everyone is going to be good at business. My wife is the best person I know, neck and neck with my mother, but I wouldn't want either of them running my business. Remember that if you follow your dream of being an entrepreneur and you don't make it, there's no shame in that. Not everyone has the talent to run a business. You read earlier about Abraham Lincoln. He failed in business several times, yet he made *Biography*'s list of one of the hundred most important figures of the last millennium. He was a great man who was not good at business. Conversely, if you do succeed and someday you drive a Porsche to work and have a nine-bedroom house, it doesn't give you the right to treat others differently. I've unfortunately seen some people with money who treat those of lesser net worth as subhuman. My wife worked for a boss who treated all of his employees like they were worthless. I also knew of a married couple who were both lawyers. They literally locked their housekeeper in the house because they didn't trust her with the combination to the house's security alarm. If they went away for the weekend, she couldn't even go into the backyard. Is that the way to treat people? If it is, they can keep their money.

I figure it this way—I don't know what will eventually happen to me. I believe I will be very successful, but I don't have a crystal ball. The important thing is that I am out there trying. I'm living my dream. And if I do fulfill my dreams, I won't forget why I embarked on them in the first place: to create something out of nothing that is all my own. If I don't make it, I have several other roles in life besides business owner that are more important such as father, husband, brother, and good neighbor. If I succeed in those roles, I will be a success.

Good luck with your endeavors. May you fulfill all of your dreams.

"That man is a success who has lived well, laughed often and loved much; who has gained the respect of intelligent men and the love of children; who has filled his niche and accomplished his task; who leaves the world better than he found it whether by a perfect poem or a rescued soul; who never lacked appreciation of earth's beauty or failed to express it; who looked for the best in others and gave the best he had." —Robert Louis Stevenson

---

INDEX

A

A&P, 87
Accountability, 15-16, 44
Accountants, 156
Adams, Franklin P., 121
Adjectives, 50
Adversity, 89-91
Advertising, 51, 95-98
Advisors, 155-156
Amazon.com, 96
American Airlines, 20
Apple Computer Company, 110
Aristotle, 133
Armstrong, Martin A., Jr., 24
Arnold, Oren, 103
Art of War, The, 7
Associations, 158-159
Atari, 110

B

Bach, Richard, 63
Baldry, W. Burton, 33
Bally's Entertainment, 23, 30
Beatles, The (music group), 94
Belief, 44
Bell, Alexander Graham, 94, 117
BellSouth, 6
Ben & Jerry's, 26
Ben & Jerry's Foundation, 26
Bergen, Edgar, 125
Berra, Yogi, 65
Bismarck, 93
Boeing, 20
Books on tape, 123
Bootstrappers, 155
Bowerman, Bill, 94, 110
Brandeis, Louis D., 61
Buck, Pearl, 89
Burke, Jim, 43
Bush, George W., 157

Business plan, 65-67
Business Start-Ups, 4

C

C&S Mystery Shoppers, Inc., 2-5, 48,
 111, 147-148
Carnegie, Andrew, 9, 144-145
Carnegie, Dale, 151
Carnegie Steel Co., 145
Chamber of commerce, 158
Chess, 119-120
Churchill, Winston, 42, 43, 63
Cippolone v. Liggett, 30
Clancy, Tom, 104
Clinton, William Jefferson, 27
Communication skills, 42-43, 137-141
Communication style, 139-140
Competitiveness, 17-21, 23-24
Complaints, 84
Confucius, 93
Consultants, 155-156
Contingencies, 75-77
Costs, 76, 88
Courtesy, 83
Creative thinking, 115-118
Credibility, 51
Crisis management, 15
Criticism, 158
Cummings, E. E., 104
Custer, George, 145
Customer identification, 99-101
Customer service, 2, 79-84

D

Dawes, Chester L., 94
Decca Recording Company, 94
Deception. *See* Dishonesty
Decision making, 12, 13-14
Decisiveness, 43-44
Delegating, 44-45, 69-71, 73

CONTACT INFORMATION:

Mark Csordos
3606 Park Avenue
Edison, NJ 08820
732.766.5913
csordos@aol.com
www.markcsordos.com

DATE DUE

DEC - 2010			

Demco